ARTS & CRAFTS MASTERPIECES

Introduction by Beth Dunlop

The three buildings in this volume – two churches and an art school – inspire superlatives. Each building epitomizes the work of its designer, and the 'art' of architecture; each is considered to be an ode to originality, though for different reasons. These buildings are, today, objects of admiration – masterpieces, visited by students of architecture, art and craft.

The buildings cover a very short time span. Charles Rennie Mackintosh's Glasgow School of Art was begun before the turn of the twentieth century, in 1897; St Andrew's Church, Roker was completed by Edward Prior in 1905; and Bernard Maybeck finished his work on the First Church of Christ, Scientist, Berkeley in 1906 (though it was not fully completed until a decade later).

These structures are all wrought by the hands of architects who were well trained and fully cognizant of the relationships between architecture, art, sculpture and craft. (Of the three, Prior was most in the vanguard of – indeed a founder of – the Arts and Crafts movement. One might consider St Andrews, Roker as a showplace of Arts and Crafts design; while it is, in general, austere, it contains work – both finishes and decoration – by Ernest Gimson, the Morris firm, Edward Burne-Jones, Macdonald Gill, and Eric Gill.) They are also linked by their powerful originality and, in the case of the buildings of both Mackintosh and Maybeck, their near-spontaneity. 'Invention is the Mother of Necessity,' wrote Allen Crawford of the Glasgow School of Art, and that adage could apply to any of the three architects or their buildings.

It is coincidental, also, that the architects share an intrinsic difficulty in being categorized. If Mackintosh, in the minds of current scholars, has grown to represent the Arts and Crafts movement in Scotland, for earlier scholars he was more difficult to classify. The great mid-twentieth-century architectural historian Henry-Russell Hitchcock, for example, stated that Mackintosh 'came nearer to possessing genius than most of the men of his generation associated with the Art Nouveau … That genius, all the same, was of so ambivalent a nature that he could seem for a few years to go along with the general stream of Continental fashion and yet, almost at the very same time, provide also a real protest against its excesses and its superficialities by the craftsman-like integrity and the almost ascetic restraint of his best work.' Nikolaus Pevsner likewise saw Mackintosh as an Art Nouveau architect on the road to modernism: 'His work such as the Glasgow School of Art of 1897–9 is distinguished by a combination of the long drawn-out nostalgic curves and the silvery-grey, lilac and rose shades of Art Nouveau with a straight, erect and resilient, uncompromisingly angular framework. Where this appears in wood, it is lacquered white. In this peculiar combination a possibility of overcoming Art Nouveau appeared, and if Mackintosh was more admired in Austria and Germany than in Britain, the reason was that these countries themselves shortly after 1900 began to search for a way out of the

jungle of Art Nouveau.' Later scholarship from the end of the century, of course, puts Mackintosh, along with many others, into an entirely separate context, that of the Arts and Crafts movement.

As for Prior, he is both considered an architect of the Edwardian era and yet takes up much of a chapter of Peter Davey's landmark book on Arts and Crafts architecture. The architectural historian Margaret Richardson, who researched the drawings of what she termed the 'Craft' architects, described Prior as eccentric, intellectual and original, noting that '[his] work is outstanding for its absence of period references. A founder member of the Art Workers' Guild, he was dedicated to its more revolutionary aims, stating his own theory – "the 'styles' are dead … such things are gone by. The savour of his art to the architect is no longer in knowledge but in experiment, in the devices of craftsmanship, in going back to the simple necessities of Building and finding in them the power of beauty."'

Furthermore, Maybeck simply seems to have mystified everyone – his contemporaries, his chroniclers and his critics. Indeed, if one is to examine most documentary histories of the first half of the twentieth century in American architecture, one would be hard pressed to find his name. His rediscovery came later – and largely in the hands of his biographer, Kenneth H. Cardwell. Maybeck was impossible to define; he termed his own work 'modern' but he was far removed from the orthodoxy of the emerging modern movement. Vincent Scully has described Maybeck as 'formalistically flexible, eclectic, and emotionally varied in his design. He was surely consciously so.' And Richard Reinhardt in his biographical essay on Maybeck (in *Three Centuries of Notable American Architects*), posited that his 'best-known buildings were unclassifiable hybrids of contemporary materials and traditional forms … the words most often used to describe Maybeck and his work – such words as eclectic, poetic, anachronistic, improvisational, romantic, neobaroque, mystical, and idiosyncratic – were certainly not the words that describe the dominant qualities of twentieth-century architecture. To the contrast, most of the words applied to Maybeck describe precisely what modern architecture is not.'

It is interesting to note that for each of the architects, the buildings in this book are essentially seminal works, even though they were designed at different points in their careers. Mackintosh was just twenty-eight when he – or rather his firm of Honeyman and Keppie – received the commission for the Glasgow School of Art, Prior was in his fifties, and Maybeck already forty-eight when he began work on the First Church of Christ, Scientist, Berkeley.

For Mackintosh, the Glasgow School of Art was his first major building, his first significant, fully-fledged work of architecture. His biographer, Alan Crawford, writes of it as a young man's design, which reveals its architect's enthusiasms. 'It has debts to Scottish tower-houses and English vernacular (especially in the centerpiece and east wing). The twin beams of the staircase and the metal discs on the front railings were inspired by Japan. The Headmaster's window and its duplicate on the east side both have the glazing set back behind the mullion, in the manner of Alexander Thomson. And there are many connections with the work of contemporary Free Style architects.'

To dwell for another minute on the question of typecasting or terminology, Crawford chose to cast the Glasgow School of Art as a Free Style building. 'The merging and interpenetrating forms of the centerpiece and east wing make it perhaps the most original in Britain. But it goes much further than any other Free Style building in a particular direction.' Crawford went on to point out the differences: 'Free Style architects design buildings, which, however loose the composition, however juxtaposed the elements, followed a single program. Here, it seems, Mackintosh did not. The School of Art is a discontinuous, fractured work, open to many interpretations. Much of its originality consists in that.'

Prior, at the age of twenty-two, was apprenticed to R. Norman Shaw and while working there was a founder of the St. George's Art Society, the precursor to the Art Workers' Guild, founded in 1884 by Prior, William Richard Lethaby, Ernest Newton, Mervyn Macartney and Gerald Horsley. The guild, according to Elizabeth Cumming and Wendy Kaplan was 'established in direct opposition to the Royal Academy, who refused to exhibit decorative art objects, and the conservative Institute of British Architects. It set out not only to raise design standards but actively to promote, like the Century Guild, "the Unity of all the Aesthetic Arts".'

While Prior was not as innovative as Mackintosh (nor, for that matter, as controversial), he was inventive. For example, in house design, he proposed a 'butterfly plan' in which two wings embraced the centre of a house as an alternative to the more typical L shape, and he patented his own deeply coloured, hand-made glass (called 'Early English') for use as church windows. Indeed, though he is little known outside of Britain, and perhaps the growing cadre of scholars of the period and the movement, in St Andrew's, Roker, Prior is considered to have designed one of the finest of all Arts and Crafts churches. Margaret Richardson points out that the church grew to be regarded as one of the best churches of the twentieth century. She said: 'The design for Roker church is highly original: the windows and tower have the generalized appearance of Gothic, but in their details are quite new. All the curves in the tracery are straightened out to become simple diagonals of stone. It was built of rough, local grey stone … The interior is one primitive space. An open timber roof is supported on great transverse arches resting on paired hexagonal columns which form a passageway between them and the walls.' Still, its originality possessed an intricacy – one that requires study and inspection. Peter Davey points out that though the placement of the 'solid castellated tower' over the chancel is a certain departure from the church's medieval antecedents, 'closer inspection reveals many

subtle innovations'. Among them, he points out the way in which the buttresses are carved out of the wall and the way in which the windows 'have all the curves of traditional tracery straightened out to become simple diagonals of stone supported on unadorned polygonal mullions'. Davey also shows that many of Prior's innovations are simply ingenious: 'The nave buttresses are cut off virtually in mid-air just above head height and their inner edges are supported on simple hexagonal columns. This allows a low aisle or passageway between the columns and the wall – the cave effect is enhanced by these little tunnels under the buttresses which allow access to the northern and southern ends of the pews.'

The building techniques were also novel – arches of reinforced concrete, for example, used at a time when concrete was not common to construction; if the construction was, for its time, avant-garde, the use of decoration was perhaps less so. Davey addresses that fact in talking about the participation of Gimson, Burne-Jones, Macdonald, the Gill brothers and the Morris firm, saying: '… that their work is to be found in a building which incorporated some of the most up-to-date technology may seem to us to be incongruous, but for Prior, there was no inconsistency: he wanted to use the best craftsmanship, the best techniques and the best local materials to create a noble place of worship for the people of his age.'

That notion of a noble place of worship brings us to Maybeck. Though schooled in the classical principles taught at the Ecole des Beaux Arts in Paris (in which he studied at the age of nineteen), Maybeck also read John Ruskin and Viollet-le-Duc, thus coming to balance out the two often-diverging worlds dominating architecture at the end of the nineteenth century. The First Church of Christ, Scientist, Berkeley is considered one of his most important – if not the most important – designs. Yet as William Jordy pointed out in his chapters on Maybeck in *American Buildings and their Architects*, 'The unalerted walking along the entrance front on Dwight Way toward the Bowditch Street corner on which the church stands might still pass it by without particular notice. The building appears by fragments, partly because of planting, partly because of the organization of the composition, and partly because of its crowded situation on a restricted site that gives no opportunity to back away from it and take it in as a whole.'

Indeed – not unlike the Glasgow School of Art and St Andrew's, Roker – it is a building that must be appreciated as a totality. Edward R. Bosley here points out that Maybeck, in the church 'provides a rare look inside the rich expansive totality of man … its interior orchestrates aspects of our collective nature, offering such examples as the intimate sanctity of a Medieval chapel, the common-sense pragmatism of a modern factory, the thundering exuberance of Romantic opera, the rustic beauty of a fireside folk song'. A key innovation in this church was Maybeck's use of ordinary, even industrial materials, and their transformation from mundane to sublime. Maybeck's biographer, Kenneth Cardwell,

wrote of this achievement in admiring terms: 'Only the genius and perseverance of the architect made the materials usually associated with factories and utilitarian building appropriate and in harmony with the edifice'. Maybeck himself put it even more simply, saying, 'We tried to fit the clothes to the man'.

It is ironic that each of the buildings in this book – particularly in the cases of Glasgow School of Art and First Church of Christ, Scientist, Berkeley – were less than fully appreciated in their own time and revered, almost as shrines, today. 'How astonished Mackintosh's Glasgow contemporaries would be if they could return to the School of Art today and see the flocks of reverential pilgrims that come from all over the world to worship at the shrine of the master,' Mark Girouard stated in an essay written in conjunction with the 1996 exhibition of Mackintosh's work. Also in that catalogue, Wendy Kaplan noted that Mackintosh was 'ridiculed and rejected by English critics at the 1896 Arts and Crafts Exhibition Society Show' (though embraced just years later in a similar exhibition held by Vienna Secessionists). Later scholars, Kaplan said, gave Mackintosh a place in the development of modernism but offered a monolithic view of his work, a view in service of a singular idea. Instead, Kaplan pointed out, there is a more embracing picture to be painted of a 'multifaceted Mackintosh, whose passion for decoration, colour, discontinuity, and sensuality in design does not negate his white abstractions so loved by modernists. Rather, the full recognition of all these qualities produces a more complex and mysterious portrait than the old myth – a story much richer and more full of contradiction.'

Likewise, for many years, fame eluded Maybeck outside of a comparatively small circle of admirers and aficionados. Cardwell writes of his chance encounter with the then aging architect, which led to a friendship and ultimately a biography. Without Cardwell's work, much less would be known of the man. John Burchard and Albert Bush-Brown point out (in *The Architecture of America: A Social and Cultural History*) that buildings such as the First Church of Christ, Scientist, Berkeley were not admired in their own time, Maybeck's church not warranting a mention in architectural histories in the mid-twentieth century. Later, however, the building was being noted. According to G.E. Kidder-Smith's description in his three-volume inventory of American architecture: 'On first entering this church one must pause and move slowly, for its subtle ambience unfolds with measured grace … The answer to its excellence is found in the triumphant mantle of the overall interior and in the transcendency of its unity, not the assemblage of its parts. Maybeck synthesized completely the "oneness" mandate, which the church's building committee had given him. The auditorium is so artfully woven together, one forgets that whispers of the Byzantine, the Gothic, Art Nouveau, and the Japanese – to name the most prominent – are all apparent.' By the end of the twentieth century the pendulum of appreciation had swung the other way.

Edward Prior
St Andrew's Church
Roker, Sunderland 1905

Trevor Garnham

Photography
Martin Charles; cover detail
also by Martin Charles
Drawings
Hetta Hunloke

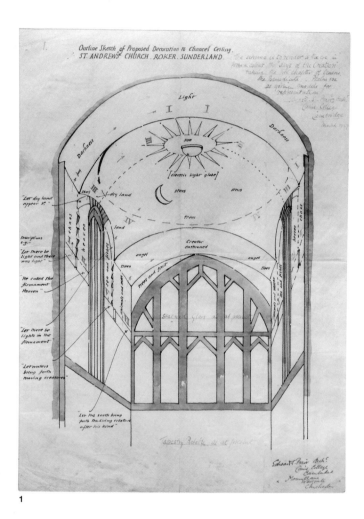

1

In the beginning

'Let there be light and there was light'. Edward Prior took the Biblical myth of Creation, set in motion with these words, for his theme to decorate the chancel of St Andrew's Church, Roker. The sketch he made for this locates quotations from Genesis within a general scheme for depicting heaven and earth as a completed 'garden of delight'. Prior's design was executed in egg tempera by MacDonald Gill (the brother of Eric Gill) who rendered this vision of an Earthly Paradise with a childlike naivety – every tree, every leaf, every fruit, all the fish in the sea, birds of the air, and beasts on the land are painted in single colour with a clear outline.[1]

This is the only decorated surface in the church. Its rich, warm colours and accessible imagery appears in stark contrast to the building itself, which is brutally severe and unrelieved by ornament. It seems almost as if Prior curtailed the Creation story at the point where Adam and Eve walked in the garden in their innocence so that no moral lesson is introduced other than, by inference, the Fall. Its central message is that mankind, driven from Paradise, must 'earn thy bread with the sweat of thy brow'. Redemption through work has been a perennial lesson of the Church. But the meaning of work had taken on a particular significance for architecture during the second half of the nineteenth century following the theories of Ruskin and Morris. They had identified the profound importance of the 'thinking hand' in craftwork and the grave threat posed by industrial production.

The Arts and Crafts movement attempted to implement the precepts of these two men and Prior was instrumental in establishing an Arts and Crafts architecture. Of all movements it is least helpful to think of this one as a 'style'. At the end of a century domi-nated by style revivalism, Arts and Crafts advocates were united by their conviction that architecture could only become a living art if it disregarded superficial motifs of style and drawn arrangements of revived histori-cal forms. As late as 1901, Prior could remark upon 'an indiscriminate copying of Byzantine, Romanesque, Italian and Indian church models all at the same time … Surely the pulse of style-worship is failing when its taste knows not what it likes.'[2] All these styles, busily competing as the new century dawned, demonstrated to Prior that any architecture conceived as a style carried no conviction. Arts and Crafts architects believed that a living architecture could only arise by thinking beyond style to the basis in work – materials and techniques.

Arts and Crafts architecture can be either soft or hard – either comforting and familiar, with small-scale spaces and refined detail-ing, as in the works of Baillie Scott, Gimson or Parker and Unwin, or a sterner architec-ture, such as Lethaby's and Prior's, responding to the rationalism of the age. Of all Prior's buildings, St Andrew's is the sternest – raw, elemental, uncompromising. Much of his architecture does not bear this stamp, but during his career certain situa-tions seemed to arise that encouraged him to explore a fascination with beginnings or first causes; the original forms, the texture left on materials by the tools. Perhaps Prior's encounter with industrial Sunderland engendered both awe at the sheer power of nineteenth-century engineering mixed with anger at the degenerative appearance of the industrialised world, prompting him to produce, in many ways, his most radical design. Although Pevsner labels St Andrew's 'neo Gothic', closer inspection reveals an almost total absence of any par-ticular stylistic points of reference.[3] It is as if Prior wished to strip away the veils of style

2

to reveal the basis of a building in work; the hard labour of quarrying and cutting stone in particular. In refusing to let any familiar ornamental motifs blunt this recognition, perhaps he hoped that the congregation might grasp, and find support in, the lesson of original man's summons to redemption through work combined with faith.

'A healthy mind in a healthy body'

Edward Schroeder Prior was born on 4 June 1852 in Greenwich, the son of John Venn Prior, a barrister in the Chancery Division. His father died when Edward was 10 years old, and his mother took the the family to Harrow where widows' sons did not have to pay school fees in some circumstances.[4] From Harrow, he went to Gonville and Caius at Cambridge in 1870. He represented his university in the hurdles, long jump and high jump, the last an event in which he became the British amateur champion in 1872. On leaving university in 1874, he became an articled pupil to Richard Norman Shaw. Shaw shot rapidly to eminence in the early 1870s following the success of his 'spectacular perspectives' shown at the Royal Academy exhibitions.[5] In the late 1870s and through the 80s, Shaw brought together many brilliant young architects who were to make their mark, along with Prior, in the Arts and Crafts movement: Ernest Newton, Gerald Horsley, Mervyn Macartney, William Lethaby, Arthur Keen, Sydney Barnsley and Robert Weir Schultz. Pupils were articled for three years before becoming assistants, firstly learning to measure up buildings and then to draw the one-eighth inch scale plans and elevations that formed the basis of practice.

Shaw usually sent his pupils to the Royal Academy schools, and many also attended the Architectural Association Class of Design in the evening but, oddly, Prior registered for neither.[6] Eventually, pupils took responsibility for co-ordinating information on a particular project and Shaw often permitted them to design detail aspects. At the end of his articled period, Prior found himself immersed in actual building as clerk of works to St Margaret's, Ilkley (1877), where he designed some of the fittings.[7] After leaving, Prior continued to work with Shaw on an occasional basis. He made designs for houses in 'a system of concrete construction in which external walls were formed of precast slabs moulded and coloured to simulate brickwork, weather-tiling or half-timber work.'[8] These were produced for a builder often used by Shaw, W H Lascelles, who patented this system of concrete construction illustrated in Shaw's two books of *Sketches for Cottages* published in 1878 and 1882.

Prior's Cambridge background made him rather different from others trained in the office, but Shaw considered him to be 'perhaps the most gifted pupil of them all.'[9] Having learnt from the best possible master, it was perhaps Prior's intellectual nature that gave the peculiar stamp to his own work as an architect, and ultimately led him back to the seat of his learning when he became Slade Professor at Cambridge in 1912. Blomfield, who knew him well, described Prior as combatively argumentative, but always with a twinkle in his eye revealing that it was points of principle and logic he was attacking, not personalities.[10]

Early works

Prior set up on his own in 1880, helped by Shaw's customary gift of a commission or two. The largest, Carr Manor near Leeds, involved extensive remodelling to produce a solid, vernacular-looking stone house dominated by its three-gabled front, possibly influenced by Webb's nearby Rounton Grange.[11] St Peter's Kelsale in Suffolk was a

3

4

5

6

7

restoration which Prior may already have worked on for Shaw.[12] He took an office at 17 Southampton Street (now Southampton Place) and leased a house at Iver, Buckinghamshire, befitting his status as gentleman-architect. Somewhat curiously, he remained living with his mother at the family home in Harrow, circumstances which were to provide considerable work for his emerging practice. He built The Red House (1883–4) for his eldest brother; St Mary's Mission Hall (1883–4) for the local Temperance Society in which his brother was active; a speculative row of four houses, Middle Road Terrace (1887); Manor Lodge (1883–4); and a series of buildings for his old school – Harrow School Laundry, Laundry Superintendent's House and Workers' Dining Hall (1887–9), funded with a loan from a building society managed by his brother, a Billiard Room (1889) and the School Music Room (1890–91). All red brick buildings, showing the legacy of Shaw's Queen Anne style, these formed part of the architectural mainstream led by George and Peto. Drawing its inspiration from the Low Countries, this period marked a lighthearted interval between the Battle of the Styles and the polemical phase of Arts and Crafts.

Another source of work was his mother's family who lived in and around Bridport, Dorset. The town had lost all its old trades to the railway (even its name had to be changed to 'West Bay' on the GWR's insistence) and Prior's projects formed part of an attempt to relaunch it as a resort – two cousins were on the Board of the West Bay Building Company. His first project for Lodging Houses, Hotel and the Lost Sailor Inn (c1883) was not built, but, much simplified, it became Prior's well-known, craggy Pier Terrace (1884–5). His later, very radical project for the West Bay Club, Bath and Promenade (1894) also remained unbuilt. In

between, he had repaired St Mary's, Burton Bradstock (his cousin was vicar), designed with William Lethaby a new south window for St John the Baptist, Symondsbury (1885 – Prior married the vicar's daughter there the same year), and the new Holy Trinity Church, Bothenhampton (1884–9) just one mile from Bridport.[13] Its unusual structure Prior later adapted for St. Andrew's.

His Cambridge connections, and his brother Charles, a Fellow of Trinity, proved to be a further source of work – a series of college alterations, new houses for tutors and Mission Halls for Pembroke College, culminating in the curiously Gothic Henry Martyn Hall (1885–9) and the surprisingly Baroque Cambridge Medical School (1899–1904). It is tempting to see this early body of work as Prior mastering the trade before he found his own radical manner exemplified in The Barn (1896–97), Kelling Place (1903–05) and St Andrew's. But this would be to over-simplify because the last phase of his practice is dominated by quiet, modest houses, such as The Small House, Levant (1909), The Oaks, near Goudhurst, Kent (1910), Windacres, Guildford (1911) and Greystones, Highcliffe, Dorset (1911–13).

In contrast with this little-known body of work, his handful of radical buildings come across as rigorous, logical explorations of intellectual propositions being formulated in the circle of Arts and Crafts architects. Whereas others in the group might keep a tight visual, compositional control over their designs on the drawing board, Prior's intellectual curiosity seems to have driven him to unfold further ideas that generated a project guided not by style but uncompromising logic, an approach that produced buildings that often appear ungainly, even puzzling, but of great originality. The catalyst seems to have been his contact with the ideas of William Morris.

8 Holy Trinity Church, Bothenhampton (1884–9). The bell tower shown in Prior's sketch was not built. The structural system of transverse masonry arches developed here was redeployed for the much larger St Andrew's.

9, 10 Prior's unexecuted, radical designs for a club comprising swimming baths, tea room, shops, library, smoking and reading rooms. One of several designs he made for the West Bay Building Company that was attempting to transform Bridport into a resort.

11, 12 The Henry Martyn Hall (1885–9) and the Cambridge Medical School (1899–1904). Two of a number of projects Prior built in Cambridge where his brother was a Fellow of Trinity College.

8

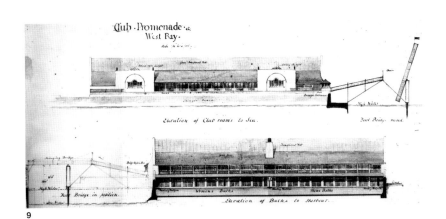

9

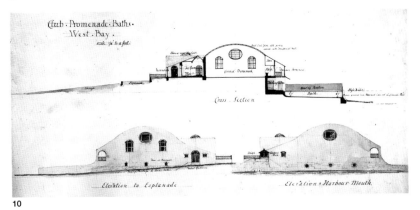

10

11

12

15

13

14

The Art-Workers' Guild

Prior remained close to Shaw's assistants throughout the 1880s and had a significant role in establishing the Art-Workers' Guild, which became the forum for the Arts and Crafts movement. He was on the committee of the St George's Art Society, an informal group drawn almost exclusively from Shaw's office – Newton, Macartney, Horsley, Lethaby and E J May completed the committee – which met regularly in the shadow of Hawksmoor's Bloomsbury church.[14] By 1883, the group had decided that bringing art and architecture together was the key to reviving architecture. Shaw lent support, writing to them that 'If Architecture in England was missing its way it was for the young men to bring her back from professionalism. The Architects of this generation must … knock at the door of Art until they are admitted.'[15]

If we detect a note of equivocation here, it is perhaps because Shaw's work began to take a rather different direction from that of his radical pupils during the 1880s – Shaw towards classicism, the younger men away from codified styles, looking instead to the vernacular for forms resulting from the meeting of materials and workmanship. This issue came to a head in 1884. Robert Kerr, founder of the AA, wrote an article critical of contemporary architecture, calling it an art of 'draughtsmanship, or sketchmanship, regarded as a delightful but delusive sleight of hand, … careless and vague in detail.'[16] Kerr held Shaw responsible for this 'scene painting', a criticism which may have played a part in Shaw turning to classicism for, what Kerr called, 'the nobler qualities' of architecture.

The inspiration for Prior's circle came from William Morris disseminating his ideas on art, handwork and architecture in the 1880s. The decisive moves made by Morris

were to disengage Ruskin's linking of handwork with Christian moral sentiments, and to recognize that Ruskin's higher aims for art would require some preliminary groundwork. There is a passage in Ruskin's *Lectures on Art and Architecture* where he acknowledges the need for sound and convenient building as a preliminary to architecture, that could stand as a text for the Arts and Crafts movement:

It indeed will generally be found that the edifice designed with this masculine reference to utility, will have a charm about it, otherwise unattainable, just as a ship constructed with simple reference to its service against powers of wind and wave, turns out one of the loveliest things that humans produce.[17]

Morris set out to revive the crafts with his own hands as well as words, but just how his example could be extended to architecture became a preoccupation of Shaw's assistants. To explore this they circulated a prospectus, which Prior wrote, inviting artists and architects to join together.

Architects who feel with us that commercial views have long discredited our Art must desire a return to an association with other Art-workers in a way that existing Architectural societies give no chance of attaining.[18]

From Prior's account we learn that the first meeting in response to this was held on 18 January 1884. An indication of Prior's commitment to Morris's ideals came when he proposed replacing 'Artists and Handicraftsmen' in a motion put by Christopher Day with, '… "Handicraftsmen and Designers in the Arts", and this, seconded by Day, was carried unanimously'.[19]

In replacing 'Artist' with 'Designers in the Arts', Prior stresses the doing of things over the broader notion of 'Artist', which could be construed as sensibility more than activity. Prior did much the same in the ensuing discussion on what might be the new Society's name. A succession of names were aired which ended with 'Prior proposing "The Art-Workers' Guild", this was carried.'[20] In formulating this name, stressing work and alluding to traditions of quality control in handicrafts, we see how persuasive Prior was, how he directed Arts and Crafts architecture away from artistic sketchmanship to workmanship, and how deeply he had imbibed Morris's views. This can be explored by examining Prior's first published writing.

'Texture as a Quality of Art and a Condition for Architecture'

A detailed account of this paper given in 1889 at the Edinburgh Art Congress is proposed here, first because it is Prior's first public pronouncement, and secondly, because it is such a little-known, but illuminating, text which helps us better to understand the curious originality of his work that followed. Prior's work tends to be known by comparison and contrast with that of his peers; looking at a single building in detail presents an opportunity to explore his work from within, to see how St Andrew's might be a response to questions raised in his writing.

The National Association for the Advancement of Art in Relation to Industry had been formed in 1888. Its genesis seems to have been bound up with the great success of the first Arts and Crafts Exhibition Society's show that autumn.[21] Morris was President of the National Association and both gave the presidential address – 'The Arts and Crafts of Today' – and chaired the session at which Prior read his paper.[22]

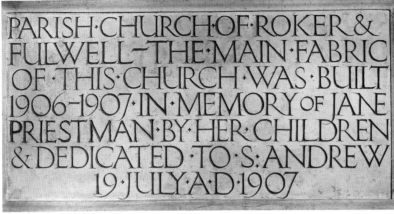

16

13, 14 Kelling Place (later Home Place), Holt, Norfolk (1903–5), entrance and site plan. Prior in his most radical Arts and Crafts idiom; 'butterfly' plan, concrete walls and floors, most materials obtained by digging a sunken garden.

15 Pier Terrace, West Bay, Bridport, Dorset (1884–5).
16 Memorial tablet in porch at St Andrew's carved by Eric Gill. Gill's promise had been spotted by William Lethaby who diverted him from architecture to lettering during his studies at the Central School of Arts and Crafts.

Prior begins by following Morris in dealing 'not only or chiefly with domes or with palaces, … the Eiffel Tower or Bridge of Forth', but defining architecture as 'common roadside building, village church and shop and cottage, farm sheds and garden walls, pathways set with quickest hedge or sharpened yew. In these familiar things a nation's architecture is shown, the more completely that they are so common and familiar.'[23]

He moves on to criticize contemporary architecture for ignoring texture. Texture, he says, 'has an acknowledged value in painting and sculpture', but is overlooked by architects or unobtainable under the system whereby 'the so-called designer dictates his purpose to the executant'.[24] For Prior, however, texture in architecture means more than 'a condition of material surface':

I would define this quality as that property of surfaces which affects our sense of sight and yet is neither definite form nor definite colour, but would ask you to perceive that what at a nearer, or under a more particular, view is form and decoration, may become at a further distance, or under a comprehensive view, this quality of Texture, but that it does so only when the colour and form have ceased to be recognised as colour or form, when they no longer have the essential effects of these properties.[25]

This is not an easy passage to follow, but its meaning is not unlike that propounded more recently by David Pye in his book *The Nature of Design*; that good design is the manipulation of surface and form to give interest to the eye at every interval from close quarters to distance. Prior seems to be suggesting that architects turn away from historical associations in design and implement instead those qualities found and enjoyed in, for example, a tree – distantly seen as sil-

houette and form, more closely as structure, detail and surface quality:

There are Nature's own Textures for us to use, or we may borrow from her, and show the grain and figure of her woods, the ordered roughness of her crystallisations in granite or sandstone, or the veinings of her marbles … Then, as evidence of our delight in Texture, we may leave our wood or stone as it comes from the chisel or the saw, to show the fracture that the tool has made, the tokens of its struggle with granite or stubborn oak. So our plaster may show the impress of the loving hand that laid it, our iron will seem to ring under the hammer that shaped it. Then of great value are our jointings of brick and stone, the piercing of our woodwork, the coursing of our slates and tiles. With these we may weave a lace-work over roof and wall and floor. More deliberate are rustications, diapers, and pattern-work, our enrichments, flutings, egg and tongue and dentil courses. These though designed, become merely Texture, when the particularity of their form is obliterated by distance, or fused by the imagination. At a still further distance the larger architectural features themselves – such as windows and piers, pinnacles and buttresses – merge into an undistinguished variegation of surface. Herein lies boundless opportunities for achieving the harmonies of Texture; and so we may provide, that from the first view of even the humblest building, this pleasant Texture should lead on by nearer approach to pleasant detail – itself well textured – and so step by step to the last limits of sight, each step revealing a further veil to be lifted, a further mystery of beauty to be solved.[26]

Prior's conception of texture might be interpreted as his search for a legitimate ground for architecture, enabling him to sidestep the fruitless arguments about appropriate

style. While this was a fairly broad aim of Arts and Crafts architects, Prior's trained mind (very few architects at this time went to university) pursued this search a good deal further:

It is a commonplace that art goes to Nature to learn the harmonies of form and colour … Beauty seems to be produced in the universe spontaneously. This is but to say in other words that man, as a part of Nature, must have the faculties to find her agreeable to him; his pulses must beat to the rhythm of her heart, his song must be in the key to her symphonies … Man can have no other source for his ideas of the good.[27]

This idea that Nature is the source of the good and the beautiful was, as Prior acknowledged, a commonplace of late nineteenth-century thought. In his essay entitled 'The Revival of Architecture', Morris had specifically linked the revival with the 'romantic school in literature'.[28] From its beginning in the Lyrical Ballads of Wordsworth and Coleridge, the idea had taken hold that before the Industrial Revolution, ordinary people engaged in everyday lives close to Nature had instinctively produced things of beauty. Wordsworth, for example, sought to revitalise poetry by observing 'the incidents of common life' expressed in 'the real language of men'.[29] Coleridge gave the clearest philosophical expression to this romantic intuition of man's essential bond with nature. He upheld imagination in opposition to the prevailing empirical view of mind which saw thinking as an essentially aggregative act – collecting, sorting, re-combining sense impressions. Defining this as 'fancy', Coleridge believed there also to be an active, originating power at work in the act of thinking, which he called Imagination. This unique

17

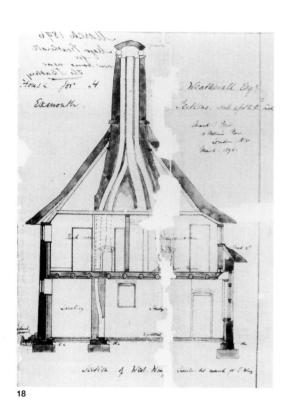

18

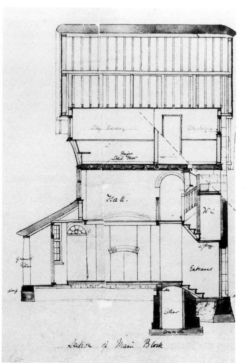

19

attribute of humanity was 'the living Power and prime Agent of all human Perception', he wrote, and 'a repetition in the finite mind of the eternal act of creation'.[30]

It was a short step from Wordsworth's shepherd and cottager to Ruskin's mythical medieval mason. Morris aimed only to bring this down to earth once more, seeing imaginative work in 'thoroughly good, ordinary country buildings, built of the mere country materials, very often of the mere stones out of the fields.'[31] Ruskin's perception of nature was much modified by his evangelism, such that nature appeared to him as God's 'second book' from which the mason could draw inspiration and express faith in his work.[32] Morris's view of nature was secular and more humble, seeing it as the face of the 'homely' earth laboured over by men in sympathy with it, an attitude to things implicit in the crafts. This had become a broad tradition by Prior's time – 'culture' and the 'thinking hand' set up in opposition to utilitarian philosophy and industrial production. Like Morris, he looked to vernacular buildings, but rather than tradition refining detail and form, Prior stressed the raw material presence, the 'beautiful harmonies of Texture, … the rough burnt brick, the rough burnt tile, the handshaped timber and the hand-cast plaster, thatch and tarred boarding, lead lattice, and bubbled glass, traceries of wrought iron, incrustations of moulded lead.'[33] The interesting thing is how elemental Prior's illustrations of texture to be found in Nature are:

The forces of the atmosphere, 'wind and storm, snow and vapour', shape out the solid earth, carving it all into valley and ridge, furrowing each valley with a thousand ravines and every ravine with a thousand chanellings. As the tide passes from the level sands it leaves the expanse ribbed and rippled into the likeness of its multitudinous seas. Every leaf that grows is veined, or blotched, or mottled, every stalk is ribbed, or hairy, or shaggy with scales. Everywhere there is gradation, everywhere dislike of monotony of surface.[34]

Prior not only deepens the investigation into the sympathetic relations between man and nature, but also conjures up a picture of his radical buildings yet to come with their rough, varied and interesting surfaces. Prior hated smoothness; it was unnatural. But, unlike Morris, he saw nature not only as an agent of formation, but also of decay:

… the hand of man, may for a little while plane, smooth or polish [but], untiring Nature goes straight to work 'tamenusque recurret'. The smooth stone or slate is creased and curdled – fretted with lichen, scrolled with moss. The polished metal recovers from the unaccustomed condition as if from some molecular distemper. It crystallises afresh, shows a tarnish, or a still more subtle patina. Here, then, should be our teaching.[35]

We can see Prior, step by step, shifting architecture away from its measure in history or morality towards a condition of geology, away from both historical form and Arts and Crafts refinement through traditions of handwork towards a more rudimentary manner of dealing with material.[36] Some original observations on details continue the thrust of his argument:

Our granite must not be moulded as our metal, nor our marble as our wood. This has been well observed in ancient practice. The most accepted profile of a cornice in stone could almost exactly be reversed to form the profile of a metal standard of the best periods; and it is suggestive to observe that the first follows with curious exactness the contours

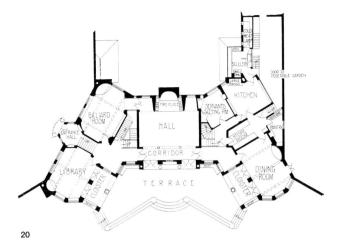

of weather-beaten limestone, and the latter almost as accurately the hollows and ridges of rust-eaten iron.[37]

This is the ultimate negation of the predominant idea that architectural ornament is a carrier of historical association. Prior vigorously pursued the fundamental ground of this position beneath time-honoured vernacular traditions reified by Morris to a more-or-less timeless geology where time's mark lies beyond human associations.

Prior concludes his paper by asking rhetorically: 'Will it be said that it was time only that gave these things their preciousness …?'[138] But he rejects this. Reciting a litany of those agents and procedures that had come to intervene between architect and the hand of the workman, he leaves his audience under no doubt that texture was there from the beginning in pre-nineteenth-century buildings and must be incorporated in contemporary design.

Radical works

The first sign of these ideas on texture informing Prior's work came in the model of a house he exhibited at the Royal Academy in 1895. In an article published contemporaneously on 'Architectural Modelling', Prior wrote that, 'architectural drawing has no sense of material, either in colour or texture'.[39] His model was like nothing seen previously. Shaped with his own hands from paraffin wax melted with turpentine, he worked in an extraordinary range of sands, dusts, chalk, coloured powders, even semolina, ground rice and mustard, to give texture.[40] Apparently a great success, the model seems to have led to the commission for The Barn which he designed early in 1896.[41] Intriguingly he was on close terms with Voysey at this time, living next door and both men practising from home. Perhaps

Voysey's lauded originality and professional success encouraged Prior to translate his own radical thoughts into design.

The Barn established Prior as an important architect; it was here that he introduced the X-shaped, or 'butterfly' plan. It is often said that Shaw's design for Chesters (1891) was the inspiration for Prior's butterfly plan, and that breaking up the mass represents a picturesque trait in the Arts and Crafts.[42] But the design can be seen to evolve from precepts in Prior's lecture on texture. From the garden-side, its appearance directly expresses the intention to break open the house and let in the sun. This pursuit of first principles in a seaside house, looking directly to the light itself, as a butterfly opens its wings to dry in the sun, seems to offer an explanation of this novel plan.[43] The broken form might also be Prior's determination to allow no specific point of recognition with the rational basis of vernacular construction. In conjunction with the heavy, textured, material presence of the built form itself, it shows how Prior tried to find his own way beyond either historical styles or vernacular logic. The wall surfaces are the very opposite of that 'smoothness' he abhorred; stone quarried locally is left roughly dressed, laid uncoursed and varied with the odd line of large boulders like rocky outcrops or a patch of smaller pebbles from the beach.

With The Barn, Prior used concrete for the first time. The floors were constructed of logs, about 9 inches in diameter, at two and a half feet centres with concrete filling between on timber lathes. Prior used concrete even more extensively in the next house he designed, Kelling Place (now Home Place), near Holt in Norfolk. Designed in 1903, this larger butterfly-plan house pursued, to its logical conclusion, the Arts and Crafts view that architecture should be wholly integrated with the landscape. For

here Prior had dug a six-foot-deep sunken garden that provided nearly all the material for the building, 'pebble facings for the walls, and ballast of all kinds for concrete, as well as a good deal of building sand and material for road making and garden paths.' Local stone and Norfolk clay tiles completed the palette for this house whose walls 'were built as concrete masses without planking, and faced with the larger pebbles … The floors were of fine concrete without steel joists, but reinforced with iron chainage'.[44] By the time this innovative, radical, yet deeply-rooted house had been completed, Prior was at work on St Andrew's.

The commission

During the course of the nineteenth century, Sunderland's population grew sixfold to reach 146,000 in 1901; shipping coal and ship-building were responsible. New docks were built, the railway came, and new industries grew up: glassmaking, potteries, ropemaking, ironworks, brewing. Three separate parishes, Bishopwearmouth, Monkwearmouth and Sunderland itself, gradually fused to become one borough. By the turn of the century, only Roker Park survived the spread of houses north of the Wear and St Andrew's Church was built to serve this new community.

Roker stands between Monkwearmouth and the sea. A church had existed at Monkwearmouth since 674 AD when Bishop Benedict Biscop, a Northumberland nobleman and a former Abbot of Canterbury who had studied in Rome, founded the Monastery of St Peter.[45] Only a part of the west porch survives, which now forms the lowest section of the tower; but this was a fortunate circumstance, for Prior was very interested in Saxon architecture and St Peter's was to provide some points of inspiration for him.[46]

23

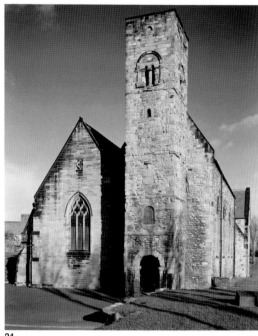

24

The need for a new church had become pressing by 1903 when the Roker and Fulwell New Church Committee was set up. Public appeals for funds began and applications were made to such bodies as the Free and Open Church Association, the Church Building Society and the Diocesan Building Society in October of that year.[47] At the same time, the Ecclesiastical Commission was approached for permission to divide the parish. This burst of activity had hardly settled when a local ship-builder, a Mr (later Sir) John Priestman, stepped in with an offer of £6,000 towards the construction of the church.[48] With his sisters, he had been looking to make a memorial to his mother (Jane Priestman is commemorated in tablets in the church carved by Eric Gill). Priestman had begun life as a draughtsman, but had risen to have his own ship-building company; he chaired several related companies and was now in a position to impose conditions on his offer, including that the further £3,000 required for the building was to be raised by 30 July 1904; the right to approve the arrangement of the new church; and that he would provide the living for a vicar of his own choice.[49] It seems that Priestman had radical views because the Committee objected to the Reverend Denis Marsh as vicar-designate and requested him 'to nominate some other clergyman – a moderate churchman – as vicar.'[50]

The Bishop of Durham, Bishop Moule, in whose diocese St Andrew's was to be built, was acquainted with Prior for he had been a Trustee of the Henry Martyn Hall.[51] Priestman had been the first man to design an iron steamer in the North-East, so one can imagine that the radically-minded ship-builder would approve of Prior, the experimental builder. We know that Prior was working on the design in 1904, for he submitted an estimate of £9,880 in December of that year.[52]

Prior had preached his radical views to men of the church six years earlier. In an address entitled 'Church building as it is and as it might be', delivered in the Jerusalem Chamber, Westminster, he attacked clergymen who insisted that their architects design in some prescribed 'correct' style. The fight against 'style' had grown throughout the 1890s reaching its climax with Lethaby's call for the term 'architecture' itself to be replaced by 'rational building'.[53] Prior's use of the phrase 'Church building' shows his allegiance to this 'art of building' (as Morris first called it), at a time when the hopes for it were fast disappearing under the emerging Grand Manner, a bombastic baroque revival that followed Queen Victoria's Golden Jubilee. This last flurry of style revivalism marked Edwardian braggadocio about Empire, Commerce and prosperous municipalities. Extravagantly practised by the like of Aston Webb, Belcher, Brydon and Mountfield, it swamped both experimental building and original essays in style. Prior concluded his call for the art of church building by contrasting it with recent practice where 'the professional architect' had been required to provide 'Ecclesiastical style, a method of building which had the form and detail of the great gothic church building which you admired. But taking a professed copy as Art, have you not denied the life of Art?'[54]

Prior's conception for St Andrew's was very straightforward. Three years before the commission, he wrote that the architect's first purpose is to provide 'a dignified distinct building dedicated to the service of the Church … At all times and in all places the greatest architecture has come into existence by the easy plan of building to a purpose.' The clergy should formulate such a programme, he said, then 'the mechanic can proceed to the erection of a simple, and

23, 24 Tower and porch from the Saxon Church of St Peter, Monkwearmouth. Prior's fascination with origins led him to employ the coupled columns from this nearby church in the structure of St Andrew's.

25. Sketch setting out plan for St Andrew's by the young Randall Wells employed by Prior as site architect.

26 Interior perspective made by Prior in 1905. Pencil and sepia washes.

27 Prior's plan of St Andrew's. The lower half shows the wall up to head height, the upper half shows nave window height.

therefore appropriate building – a simply built, and therefore dignified, cathedral.'[55]

Prior had been instructed to seat 600 and to give all the congregation a view of the altar and pulpit. This aim was in keeping with the liturgical movement putting into reverse the changes that had shaped the nineteenth-century church since the passing of the Catholic Emancipation Act of 1829. Between them, Pugin and the Ecclesiologists had curtailed the development of hall-like preaching churches which had begun after the Reformation, Pugin hoping to rekindle medieval faith and charity by returning to gothic architecture, and the Anglican movement combatting the drift to Rome or non-belief in the cities by emphasizing the sacraments and the mysteries of the church as a divine society. This had led to chancel arches, distant altar, fat gothic columns either side of narrow nave, and even the return of the altar screen. As the nineteenth century drew to a close, however, Protestants once again began to play down 'the sacrificial interpretation of the mass and emphasised its communion aspect',[56] stressing the word and breaking down the rigid dichotomy of ordained and lay person.

It is in this liturgical context that St Andrew's needs to be understood. For the striking aspect of the church is the impression made by the vast, open, uncolumned hall. Its direct simplicity affirms Prior's belief that the 'church builder' should be a 'servant' to the aspirations of the clergy, a kind of 'mechanic' to realize liturgical aims to best advantage. Mechanic here is not an inappropriate word, for the church is 52 feet wide, an extraordinary single span for a parish church. With deep, thick arches springing low from massive walls, all the congregation obtain a good view of pulpit and altar. Visibility for the altar is enhanced by the shallow chancel having its walls

26

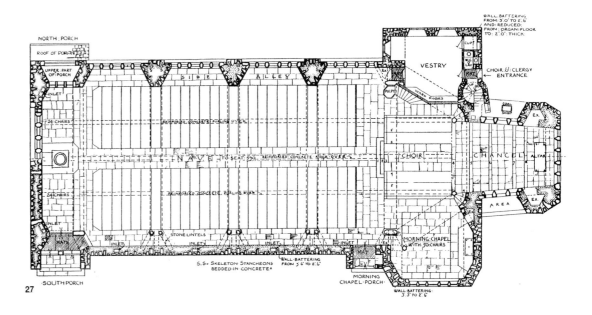

27

28

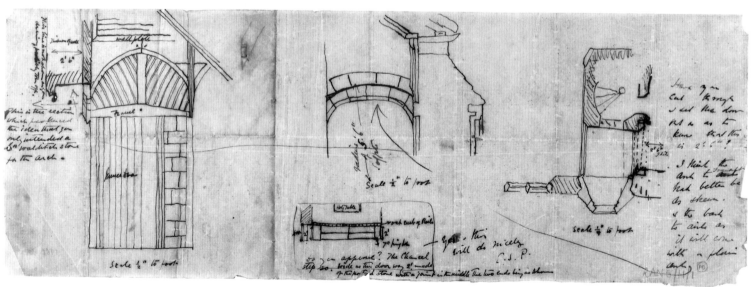

29

tapered in towards the east end. The volume of the nave, with its clear display of structure, has been likened to an upturned boat. While this does appear not unlike a ship at the moment of construction, with its keel and ribs visibly shaping the hull, it would be wrong to pursue this kind of symbolism, although the analogy might be apt for such a ship-building community. Unlike his friend Lethaby, who remained fascinated by symbolism of this kind, Prior seemed to want nothing to come between the direct expression of word and work; he proposed no symbolic structure over and above the work itself. In this he remained close to Morris, seeing in the dignity of labour sufficient and appropriate meaning to embellish the church.

To this end, Prior vigorously pruned his conception of architecture. In his inaugural lecture as Slade Professor delivered five years after St Andrew's was completed, he explained the place of historical styles in his scheme for teaching architecture: 'the teaching of these should be directed to the great creative periods. The actions of building, however complex in their results, have been in themselves few: in a broad sense the wall and the roof comprise them.'[57] Following his lead is perhaps the best way to understand how St Andrew's took shape from its straightforward conception.

The wall

The nave walls are three and a half feet thick at floor level and batter to two and a half feet at window sill height. Piers project five feet into the nave and their inner face is taken up in a shallow arch above each window. The massive buttressing piers, the thickness implied by the closing of the wall above, combine with the low-springing stone arches across the nave to produce the overriding impression of a deeply-protected interior. The uncoursed, random-rubble stone is left unplastered with only the quoins and voussoirs dressed to a flat surface; the thickness of the wall hence finds an echo in the rough, undulating surface of the stone itself.

The stone was quarried from Marsden about three miles north of the site. There was a quarry much closer on Carley Hill, Fulwell, where the same grey magnesium limestone was dug (St Andrew's is sited on the same ridge which ends 200 yards away in 50-foot-high cliffs). But Fulwell Quarry was a huge, mechanized quarry, whereas Marsden 'was worked by quarrymen with their usual tool – the scutcher, a broad bladed pickaxe, which from constant practice they [used] with freedom, yet wonderful precision'.[58] It is an unusual stone found in uneven beds of varying thickness; it does not break naturally along bedding lines but into irregular shapes. Sometimes it is hard and compact, and others it has a curious crystalline structure (in appearance like a tiny version of the Giants Causeway in Ireland) which, when dressed, looks like pumice. Consequently, it is not a stone that lends itself to precisely-rendered detail. Of course, Prior was not interested in delineating a particular style through prescribed detail. No professional purveyor of styles, he pursued his alternative view that an architect should be a mechanic by employing Randall Wells, as site architect. Wells had fulfilled the same role for him at Kelling Place, and before that at All Saints, Brockhampton for Lethaby. There is a sketch plan dated 30 January 1906 showing St Andrew's just pegged out, where Randall Wells signs himself 'resident architect'.[59]

Commencement of the work had been delayed because the Ecclesiastical Commissioners had been slow to authorize the creation of the new parish. In February 1906, the Commissioners had approved Prior's design, although they were concerned about the size of the columns supporting the tower, and also 'the columns under the arches in the nave'.[60] This criticism refers to an ingenious aspect of Prior's design. By bringing the arches down as internal buttresses, he had effectively increased the width between external walls. To maximize width for seating, he pierced through the buttresses to create side passages, transferring the weight to a pair of columns. An important Victorian church where a passage is similarly cut through interior buttresses is G F Bodley's St Augustine, Pendlebury (1874), which Prior would have known. But more interestingly, just such a detail of coupled columns exists at nearby St Peter's as a part of the western porch to the original Saxon church; we can imagine Prior's delight in using it here, providing a constant reminder of the early origins of Christian worship in the parish. Indeed, the plan form itself has Saxon connotations, for Prior argued that the 'ancient oblong chamber' with 'small square-ended sanctuary' represented 'the earliest tradition in our islands'.[61] The simple cushion capitals are like those illustrated in Lethaby's book *The Church of Sancta Sophia*. Lethaby called Romanesque 'the supremely logical building art' that had sprung from the masons' invention of the arch, which in turn encouraged them to generate 'an entirely fresh group of capitals'.[62] These Saxon and Romanesque references show that Prior's search for origins could not rest on empirical practice alone.

Randall Wells did not reply to the Commissioners' concern about the structure until January 1907, by which time the building must have been well advanced. He explained how the tower support had been strengthened by thickening the columns below and building lintels 'corbel fashion with long tails onto the walls.' 'The twin columns in the nave,' he continued, 'have been made 18" diameter and by the method of reinforcement the weight is carried by the wall behind which was thickened to 3' 0" and strengthened with two 18" x 9" skeleton staunchions'.[63] This pair of vertical staunchions 'of light angle iron, cross-braced, 15 ft high … with their ends firmly bedded in the concrete foundations',[64] helps to combat sheer force. A plan showing these suggests that, at one point in the design, the interior of the nave walls was to be left as unfaced concrete. As built, however, the wall is a more conventional construction of stone facings with a core of concrete and rubble. For its first 20 years, the chancel's walls and shallow domed ceiling was left as found when the shuttering was struck. 'They have been left in their rough state,' remarked the Reverend Denis Marsh, 'and the effect, fitting in with the architect's general idea of simplicity and freedom from machine work, is very pleasing.'[65]

A surviving sketch for the vestry entrance by Wells – with notes added by Prior – confirms what we can infer from Wells's letter, and what we know from his work with Lethaby at Brockhampton, of this working relationship between architect, site architect and mason. Prior drew the plans, section and elevations, working out in strategic terms and to some considerable detail the arrangement and appearance of the church. At one level, the building is a straightforward response to the plan serving the liturgical aims of the church; at another level, its appearance results from Prior and Wells seeking out the local stone and seeing what could be done with it. Wells would then not only supervise the work, sorting out problems as they arose, but also engage the masons in decisions about how best to use

30

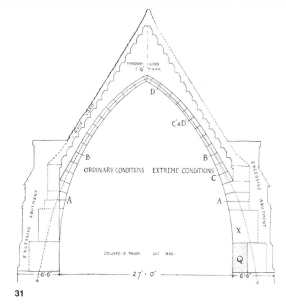

31

32

33

the stone. Jointly promoted by Prior and Lethaby, this experimental, rational, democratic way of building with stone and concrete was inspired by their historical researches into the inventive medieval mason.

The roof

It is hard to imagine now just how radical Prior's structure was. He had first explored this structural system of low-springing arches at Holy Trinity, Bothenhampton because, he said, a timber roof would creak in high winds. Although the span there is only 27 feet 6 inches, low arches springing from unbuttressed walls, having no tie from the roof structure, caused the Incorporated Church Building Society to question its stability and reject the design. There is a furious letter from Prior defending his design's stability mathematically (the maths, he says, had been reviewed by his brother Charles, the Cambridge 3rd Wrangler Lecturer and Professor Burnside, Professor of Mathematics at the Naval College, Greenwich) and by a list of precedents where stone arches formed the principal members of a roof.[66] He demonstrated that such a roof had survived for more than 600 years in the Treasury, Merton College, and that it could span as large as 39 feet 3 inches at The Hall in Mayfield, Sussex. He could also point to his own experience with Shaw, who had used a similar structure spanning 32 feet at Adcote in 1875.[67] At Bothenhampton he remained, like Shaw, otherwise close to traditional construction with pointed stone arches and oak purlins, but at St Andrew's the structure is more radical. Nevertheless, it follows the same principle, as he explained to *The Builder* using a diagram of the structural forces he had prepared for Bothenhampton. Concrete was used, he added, because

dressed stone was 'an expensive luxury in the neighbourhood'.[68]

The five massive, transverse, double-radius arches are built of carefully selected larger blocks of the Marsden stone, the quoins alternating between running across the face of the arch and into its depths. The side face of the three-foot-wide arches is the only place where the stone is coursed – following the radius line. Although this suggests that they would be stable if built of solid stone, each is, in fact, reinforced with four iron rods bedded in a concrete core.

The very deep purlins and ridge beam which span 20 feet between supporting arches are also of reinforced concrete, the shuttermarks clearly visible. No detail drawing or specification survives, but a note from Wells says they are reinforced with 'Kahn bars' which were fixed to the bars in the arches.[69] Another possibility they might have considered was to use a steel chain as at Kelling Place. It is worth noting in relation to this that the plan of the church was modified from the first drawings – where the nave walls continued directly eastwards to form the chancel – in that, as built, the corners of the chancel walls were pulled in very close to the inner face of the purlins. Thus, the mass of the chancel walls would help to restrain chains. Furthermore, massive six-foot-wide shallow arches spring obliquely from this junction with the chancel back to the nave walls, giving further restraint. Lateral restraint is similarly provided to the west wall by an equivalent arch and by halving the distance to the first transverse arch. Perhaps options were kept open as construction progressed.

Although concrete remained a very novel form of building construction, Bentley's recently completed concrete domes for Westminster Cathedral had received much publicity, prompting a debate on the role of

31 Prior's sketch section of Holy Trinity, Bothenhampton (1884–9) demonstrating the stability of this structural system which was originally rejected by the Church Building Society. The right hand part of the section shows that the thrusts remain within the structural arches (dotted lines between C C and D D) were the compressive forces to be removed by either wind suction or destruction of the roof by fire.
32 Interior view of Holy Trinity, Bothenhampton.

33 The Hall, Adcote, Shropshire (1875) by Richard Norman Shaw. The design and construction of this took place during Prior's time in Shaw's office.
34 Westminster Cathedral (1895–1903), by John Francis Bentley. This view was made before the interior was decorated when the great concrete domes and thick brick walls most impressed radical architects such as Prior and Lethaby whose book on Santa Sophia was much referred to by Bentley in the design.

concrete in architecture. Interestingly, Prior was closely involved in organizing the Seventh International Congress of Architecture which incorporated a session on 'Steel and Reinforced Concrete Construction' where calculations for 'shearing stress', adhesion of concrete to reinforcement, rusting iron, cover to reinforcement, etc, were discussed. This took place at the RIBA on 18 July 1906, when work on the walls of St Andrew's must have been well under way.[70]

The structure was described shortly after completion as 'forming an imperishable skeleton.' However, the way in which the thickness of the walls were developed, its textured surface of stone, and the way that the immense walls were hollowed to capture the play of light from the nave windows, creates an impression more of being inside some vast cellar or cave transfigured by light than a merely rational structural skeleton. The outcome of this, curiously, is an almost exact reversal of gothic architecture. A major impetus of the combined efforts of medieval master mason and monk had been to reduce the appearance of mass to line, hence the invention and elaboration of the rib, clerestory and shaft. At St Andrew's, the presence of the building's mass is emphasized by texture so that mass and light are held in a very different kind of equipoise to a gothic cathedral.[71] In this, Prior brings to a culmination an ambition shared by radical late nineteenth-century architects, to shift the definition of gothic from a historical style to gothic as a way of building. Gothic, in this way of thinking, was seen as quintessentially the art of masonry construction in which invention at the level of structure and detail resulted from a close collaboration between the conceiving mind of the architect and the 'thinking hand' of the mason.

Openings

Prior had spoken of the need to transfer something of the strength of a wall into its openings. At St Andrew's, the blunt directness of this plays a decisive part in shaping the character of the building. The windows in the nave, for example, are subdivided by mullions made of blocks of stone simply feathered away to a thin face. Transomes form cross-bracing (perhaps suggesting the St Andrew's cross), above which a pair of simply canted stones form triangles that help prop the arched opening. On the one hand, this could be seen as Randall Wells pursuing the aim for simplicity from general arrangement to detail in accepting the characteristics of the stone; on the other hand, it might be interpreted in the light of Prior's search for origins.

In his book *Eight Chapters on Medieval Art*, Prior proposed that the only way to understand the particular development of English architecture was to consider 'its special beginnings'. Acknowledging that the Norman Conquest had joined England to the Latin civilizations of Western Europe, he nevertheless contended that 'English culture had already determined its quality in pre-conquest church building, and the Saxon ancestry of our artists, if in the background for a while, asserted itself in some two or three generations.'[72]

In addition to the coupled columns, the small windows in the tower provide the clearest evidence of Prior looking back to Saxon building, for they are direct quotations from St Peter, Barton on Humber, one of the best surviving Saxon churches. With the opening straightforwardly spanned by two stones meeting at the apex (which project from the face to form a hood) these windows are very suggestive of a primitive culture fumbling towards a stone language from a timber precursor.

34

35 St Peter, Barton-on-Humber.
A Saxon church showing the
'megalithic' lintelled doorway
and 'pilaster' system that Prior
refers to in window openings and
the tracery at St Andrew's.
36 All Saints, Earl's Barton,
another Saxon church known
to Prior.

37 All Saint's Swanscombe,
Kent (1893–5) by Richard
Norman Shaw.
38 St Andrew's tower seen in
the context of the Victorian
suburb it was built to serve.
39 South elevation drawing
by Prior.

35

36

The development of this by Prior into the 'tracery' of the nave also seems to draw inspiration from the 'pilaster' treatment of the same Saxon church tower, or from another well-known Saxon church, All Saints, Earl's Barton. But by transforming the Saxon wall articulation into a tracery window inextricably associated with the gothic desire for light in the walls, Prior stubbornly refuses to allow the design to be stylistically located. More recent scholars have dubbed Saxon architecture 'megalithic' because of its incorporation of large available blocks of stone with rubble, suggestive of what one might expect from the primitive beginnings of a masonry tradition yet to evolve into the refinements of gothic.[73] Prior's nave windows have this attribute much more than Saxon architecture itself. In the chancel, the stone tracery is more elaborate for 'capitals' develop from the mason stepping back a sequence of three stones to a rectangular block. The stones springing from these 'capitals' to support the transome convey a faintly anthropomorphic suggestion of Christ hanging from the cross.

The exterior

'Church architecture, least of all, has been able to go beyond the trivial efforts of traditional picturesqueness; least of all our building has it been monumental.'[74]

Whether or not building simply and massively produces monumentality is a difficult question. But Prior certainly refuses any contrivance that might have made St Andrew's more picturesque. The massiveness of the church is enhanced by setting the nave wall back at window sill level. Probably resulting from careful adjustment of the section to bring light closer to the nave interior, the lower wall is continued upwards as buttresses that find an echo in the curious roofed 'pinnacles' above. While this might be read as a truthful allusion to the structural forces, it is even more an illusion of a stone wall much thicker than it actually is. Porches simply lean against this wall to form entrances; Saxon churches, Prior said, usually had 'no west door, but often porches projecting north and south'.[75] Lack of mediation between the scale of door and building adds to the impression of massive size.

The parapet wall is high and runs round the transepts, giving a long, low appearance to the church. Prior was familiar with those East Anglian churches – Blythburgh, Long Melford, Lavenham – that were built upon the wool trade and sit so well upon the land.[76] The most unusual aspect of St Andrew's, however, is the tower positioned above the chancel. There seem to be several interrelated explanations for this.

Although local legend has it that Prior located the tower nearest to the sea so that sailors could navigate by it, this may have been more metaphorical than literal. The Reverend Denis Marsh described it as 'a beacon for our sailor brothers', and giving 'a parting message of peace and courage, for did not Jesus come walking to the toilers on the sea?'[77] The tower, so positioned, also gives St Andrew's greater visibility from Roker Park Road, the main artery through the suburb.

In addition to these two topographical advantages, Prior seemed to be exploring a formal exercise, and possibly a moral one. From the mid-1870s, Shaw had tried to combine Bodley's new vision of the open single-volumed church with his own of a church with a central tower. A series of projects – St Margaret's, Ilkley, St Michael's, Turnham Green and All Saints, Richards Castle – culminated in All Saints, Swanscome (1893–5) where the long unified volume of nave and chancel pierces through a central tower.[78] At St Andrew's, Prior contrives a vestige of the nave roof line at the east end beyond the tower. The 80-foot-tall, square tower has four hexagonal corner towers containing ventilation shafts and stairs, where the board-marked concrete can be seen. Originally capped with tall pyramid roofs (removed because of wind damage) the corner towers are pulled together with repeated shallow arches above the belfry.

Positioning the tower over the symbolically significant chancel may have appealed on moral grounds. Prior formed the opinion that 'a square-topped, spireless tower' was an expression of 'democratic growth', and had become commonplace because 'bell-ringing was the popular sport. Tower building was in fact an exercise of popular religion itself.'[79] Once the crafts had become secretive and excessively protective in the fourteenth century, Prior believed that the democratic art of building persisted only in the small parish church characterized by its tower and house-like nave.[80] Situated over the crossing, blurring any distinction between nave and chancel, congregation and clergy, bell-ringing is thus given an elevated dignity within the overall meaning of the church here at St Andrew's.

Furnishings and fittings

The east window has stained glass, by A H Payne of Birmingham, depicting the Ascension of Christ. This event, of course, marks a new beginning in Christian doctrine, a great cycle that will end in the Day of Judgment. Below this is a tapestry depicting the visit of the three wise men to the infant Jesus. Made in William Morris's workshop at Merton, this is a copy of a painting by Burne-Jones – an apt choice for the reredos as it brings Morris, his circle and ideals into the focal point of the church. The scene depicted also introduces two images which underscore Prior's pursuit of origins, over and above the central message of Christ's

37

38

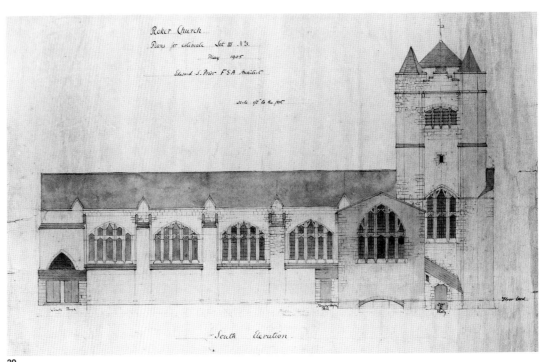

39

40

41

earthly birth. The stable is an archetypal primitive hut, like that depicted by Laugier in the eighteenth century when he tried to reformulate a legitimating ground for architecture upon its origins after the collapse of Renaissance cosmology. Furthermore, a wattle fence provides enclosure which carries a suggestion of Semper's nineteenth-century attempt to ground architecture in processes of making – firing, weaving, piling up and jointing. The hearth and woven partition were considered by Semper to be the fundamental archetypes of settlement.[81]

The furniture and panelling in the chancel were made by Ernest Gimson and mark a particularly interesting moment in Gimson's career.[82] Along with Ernest and Sydney Barnsley (who had worked in Shaw's office with Prior), Gimson had taken Morris's call to the crafts most literally, leaving London in 1892 to establish craft workshops in the Cotswolds.[83] At first, their furniture design relied heavily upon techniques learnt from a local joiner, Philip Clissett, but in 1901, Peter van der Waals joined the enterprise. Whether or not by coincidence, from this time on their furniture makes much use of chamfering a technique which originated in the wheelwright's craft where it lightened the weight of the wheel without impairing its strength. Over time, this had come to form decorative treatment of wagons. It was probably adopted for furniture by Gimson because it softened sharp corners and edges, and anticipated wear. At St Andrew's, chamfer upon chamfer produce complex decorative patterns. Prior himself designed the pews which were made by the North of England School Furnishing Company incorporating a similar, if less elaborate, technique.[84] In this way, a reminder of the dignity of work, a reference to time-honoured craft traditions, was brought inescapably close to the congregation.

Gimson also made the ebony lectern inlaid with mother-of-pearl and silver, perhaps a little too elaborate to fit easily into this setting. The cross and the candlesticks on the High Altar were also made at Gimson's Sapperton works by his blacksmith, Alfred Bucknall. These were beaten from wrought iron and lacquered to prevent rusting.

The tall back of Gimson's pews form a screen to the Lady Chapel in the south transept, a dark, stony space, dominated by the glow from Payne's stained-glass window. Taking as its text the words inscribed at the top of the window: 'Come unto me all who are heavy laden and I will give you rest', it is a further celebration of the dignity of labour. Around the central figure depicting the Christ of daily life are representations of all sorts and conditions of men and women, including the mother with her child, the workman with his tools, and a man heavy-burdened whose load is loosened as he looks upon Christ. The organ, paid for and played by Priestman, occupies the other transept.

The clear glass to the nave windows was 'manufactured according to the architect's patent method.'[185] Prior had arranged for a small glassworks, Britten and Gibson of Southwark, to produce 'Prior's Early English Glass', 'a glass with particular qualities'. As the name suggests, Prior developed his specification from a careful study of old work. Produced by blowing the molten glass into a rectangular clay mould, contact with the mould gave it a rough finish. Stretching to reach the corners of the mould, the glass becomes thin and rippled. Prior's specification called for an 'uneveness of thickness … with or without bubbles and other accidental flaws and irregularities.'[186] This lends a subtle variation to the intensity of light as it plays across the interior. The iron glazing bars were made in Priestman's shipyard.

Electric arc lights in the nave could be 'pulled up into the roof by means of a wire rope and winding apparatus at the side.'[187] The sparkling effect of light reflecting from the irregular face of the glass caused much delight. An inverted 'umbrella'-shaped copper bowl hung in the sanctuary within which a number of electric lamps shone 'onto the white dome, and so [gave] a subdued light to the altar.'[188] The bowl was perforated to give direct illumination to the tapestry. At the centre of the nave, in the space left free for entrance, is an elaborate font carved from Marsden stone by Randall Wells. A striking design, large enough to immerse a child and looking like a cauldron on four corner posts, it is carved with swirling vegetation, perhaps an allusion to early Christian Celtic art prominent in the region.

The walls to the nave are panelled to a height of 7 feet 8 inches in English oak. The boards are of uneven width, fixed with hand-made iron nails. Inset into the wall above are louvred hot-air outlets. Within the mass of the concrete wall, Prior incorporated vertical ducts that connect to a plenum system running beneath the floor to a chamber below the chancel where huge indirect radiators were located. The hot air from these was propelled by 'a Blackman electric fan … capable of pouring 700,000 cubic feet of air into the church every hour, which means that the air of the church can be completely changed every twenty minutes.'[189] The air intake is beneath the Morning Chapel, the boiler beneath the organ loft.

With all the windows having fixed lights, Prior had to rely largely on the volume of the space and hot air rising to maintain comfortable air conditions for the congregation. However, he did provide two 'doors' in the chancel which are, in fact, 'the lower openings of two ventilating shafts which rise up into the tower.'[190]

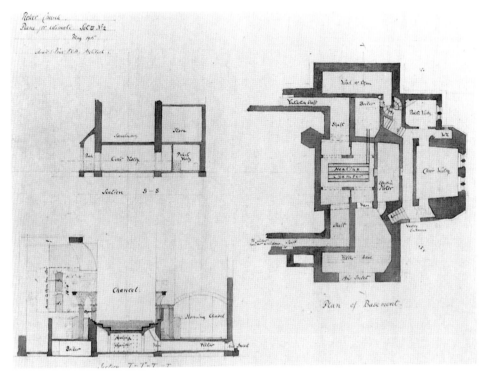

42

43

44 Inside window to tower showing mass concrete wall construction.

45 Tracery made with pairs of sloping stones that refer to Saxon gabled head window lintels.

46 Elaboration of the gabled heads to form 'proto-capitals' in the chancel.

44

45

46

47 Gabled head lintels over window in tower.

48 View showing how the massive stone arches, supported on paired columns, meet the nave wall with a passage cut through internal buttress to provide side-access to pews.

49 Underside of spiral stair to bell tower.

50 The surface of a piece of Marsden stone showing the curious coarse grain that does not lend itself to fine detailing.

48

47

49

50

51 Detail of pulpit showing
Gimson's chamfered joinery
resting on a stumpy column of
Marsden stone.

51

Rational building or mythical masonry?

With this remark we seem to be on the threshold of modernism; not only do we have a straightforwardly functional plan, a reinforced concrete structure and electric lights, but also an integrated heating and ventilation system. St Andrew's may not have been well known enough for Pevsner to incorporate it into his chain of pioneers leading to what he saw as an inevitable modernism; its 'neo-gothic' appearance would have distracted from the thrust of Pevsner's narrative. But nor could Prior be marginalized later into Pevsner's *The Anti-Rationalists*. He did, however, form one of Goodhart Rendell's collection of late nineteenth-century 'rogue architects', a label just as easily construed as marginalizing those swimming in neither mainstream, forward towards modernism, or backward to historicism. The idea of an 'English Free Style' would have been as disagreeable to Prior as 'smoothness'.

After describing the curious chancel ventilation doors, the Reverend Denis Marsh continued that 'there is a pescina fitted into the wall; that is to say a small basin and water drain, through which the water used at the Holy Communion service is poured away, so that it may return to the earth in a natural way without entering an ordinary drain.'[91] Here we see the gulf that separates our world from Prior's. His conception of the architect as a kind of 'mechanic' of 'rational building' did not presume to enclose all human endeavour within an all-embracing rationality. Prior's vision was largely shaped by that mythical medievalism that ran back through Morris and Ruskin to its roots in romanticism. A central tenet was that man's spirit must resist the triumph of materialism. It insisted upon a symbiotic relationship between man and nature. Prior's conception of 'texture' and the pursuit of the 'thinking hand' – or simply the dignity of hard labour –

in the building of St Andrew's represents a last attempt to construct such a world.

Like Lethaby, he came to measure his words on 'rational building', which was all too easily conflated with 'positivism'. Let us not forget that the character of modernism was completely unforseeable when Prior built St Andrew's. But any serious-minded man knew that 'style' was a futile response to the thrust of the age. It was to be another generation before a purely empirical view would prevail and fuse with myths and metaphors of the machine to produce a modernism of many guises that dominated the twentieth century. Now that we recognize this to have been an ideological construction rather than an evolutionary inevitable, explains why we find someone like Prior so interesting. Perhaps, like Morris, whose anger increased as he came to understand the workings of capitalism, Prior saw its imperative here in Sunderland turning small, workshop-like shipyards into industrial sites, and was driven to produce this radical, uncompromising embodiment of his vision whereby labour was dignified and made meaningful.

It is hard for us to recapture this, trapped as we are between uncritical notions of progress and 'traditions' seen to be fogeyish as this style or that. But for Prior, the concept of tradition was more subtle and complex. His pursuit of origins can help us understand how trapped we are, even as we acknowledge how trapped he was by historicism, his search for origins eventually ending up somewhere between Saxon and Norman, Romanesque and Roman. Ever oscillating between an authentic way of working and the first style, it is precisely this impossibility to see things either purely empirically or stylistically that separates Prior's world from ours and makes St Andrew's so intriguing.

Photographs

View from the south-west. The raw simplicity of the church, the rough stone, the irregular blocks making the arches, the straight-forward 'megalithic' tracery, are all manifestations of Prior's desire to involve the masons in attaining meaning from the work. Prior went along with Lethaby in arguing for radical building rather than 'architecture'.

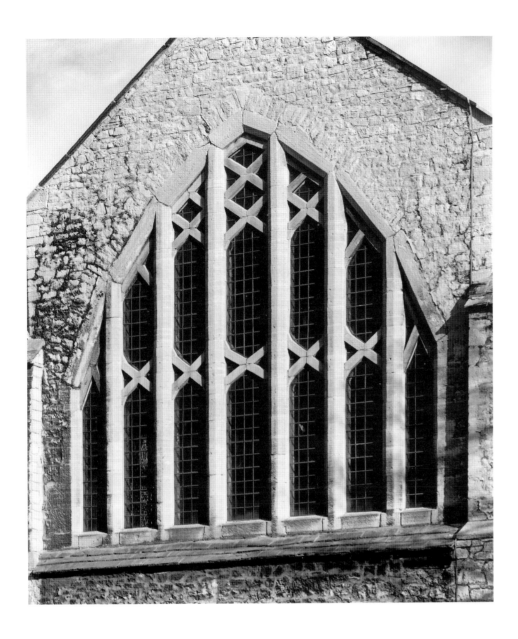

Detail of wall over south-west entry porch showing the piers projecting above the cornice adding weight to the internal buttresses below. The tracery in the west window and nave windows is both a response to the nature of the stone, its quarrying and working, and also Prior's interest in Saxon masonry. The stone cross bracing might be an allusion to the St Andrew's cross.

Prior contrived a vestige of pitched roof at the east end so that the church appears simply as a single body embracing nave and chancel that pierces the tower. The hooded windows in the stair tower derive from Saxon sources and become elaborated as a motif for the chancel tracery.

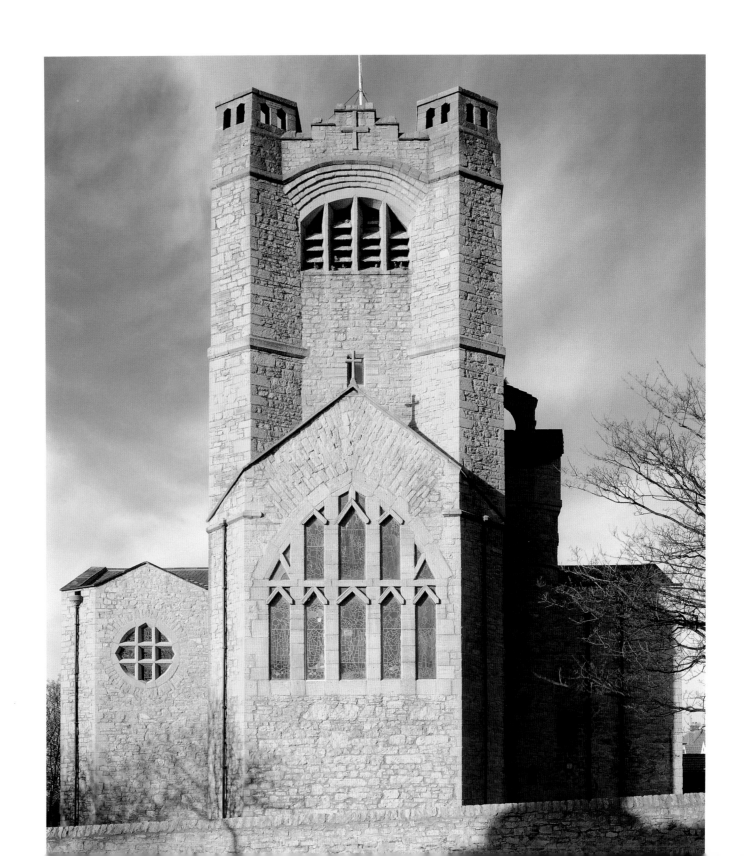

Prior believed that a square-topped spireless tower was an expression of 'democratic growth' and had developed as an English tradition because bell-ringing was a popular folk art. He turned to Saxon precedent again in providing no more than a simple lean-to porch on the south nave wall to denote entry.

The cavernous 52-foot-wide nave with its extraordinary single spanning stone arches. Each is, in fact, reinforced with four iron rods bedded in concrete that connect to reinforcing rods in the concrete purlins.

Left View into the chancel with its ceiling painted by MacDonald Gill after Prior's design. The chancel walls taper in to create a foreshortening effect that helps bring the altar seemingly closer to the congregation.

Above The organ was donated by John Priestman, principal benefactor to the church, who was also the first organist.

Right Oak panelling in uneven width boards, a detail contribution to help overcome Prior's dislike of smoothness.

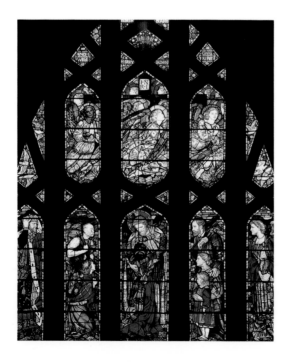

Above Chancel with panelling by Gimson. The 'door' to the ventilation shaft can be seen beside the altar.

Above left Altar hanging made in the Morris & Co workshops after a design by Burne-Jones.

Left Lady Chapel stained-glass window by A H Payne. Taking as its text 'Come unto me all who are heavy laden and I will give you rest', it celebrates the dignity of labour as represented by local trades and individuals. Apparently the 'black angel' is a result of trial firing of the glass.

Right The chancel ceiling was painted 20 years after the church had been consecrated. Prior's design took Creation as its theme, the allusion to origins chiming nicely with the stone tracery suggesting a Gothic architecture having its origins in the rudimentary 'megalithic' masonry of Saxon Britain when our first churches were built.

Above and right Details of oak choir stalls by Gimson and Barnsley. Their furniture at this time made extensive and elaborate use of chamfering. Derived from the wheelwright's craft this 'decoration' brought the message of the craftsman's contribution to design directly to the congregation.
Far right The Lady Chapel.

Prior's patented 'Early English Glass' was used throughout and makes an extraordinary contribution to the space of the church. The uneveness of thickness and irregularities encouraged in the process of making gives a subtle variation to the light as it plays across the deep stone reveals.

The coupled columns support the springing of the stone arches and allow passage along the sides of the nave. They were inspired by similar columns at the nearby Saxon church of St Peter, Monkwearmouth. The simple cushion capitals are like the first Romanesque capitals that masons developed in response to their invention of the arch.
Above Font carved from Marsden stone by A Randall Wells, the site architect.

Crosses and candlesticks by
Gimson and Barnsley's blacksmith Alfred Bucknall. Beaten
from wrought iron they are lacquered to prevent rusting. The
ebony lectern with inlaid mother-
of-pearl and silver was designed
and made by Ernest Gimson.

Mere Knolls Road

Claremont Road

Talbot Road

Park Avenue

Roker Park

North Sea

River Wear

Drawings

N

0   200m

0   500ft

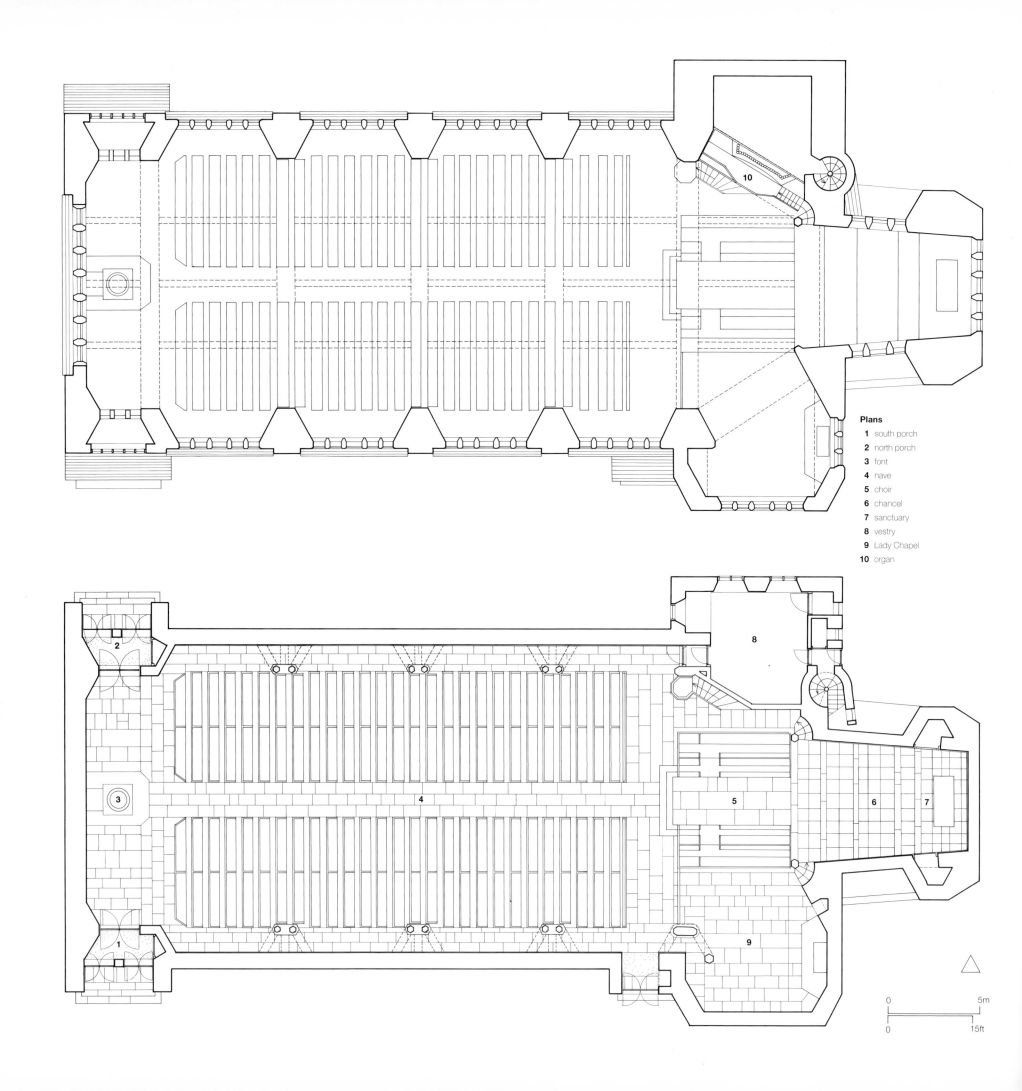

Plans

1 south porch
2 north porch
3 font
4 nave
5 choir
6 chancel
7 sanctuary
8 vestry
9 Lady Chapel
10 organ

0   5m

0   15ft

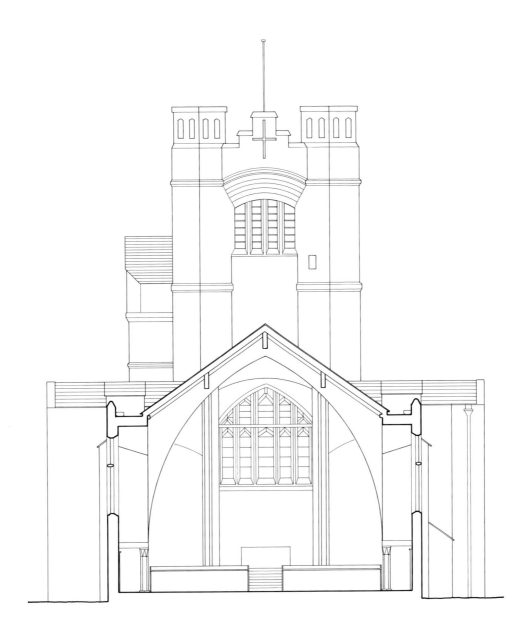

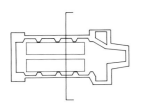

0   15m

0   15ft

Long elevation facing south

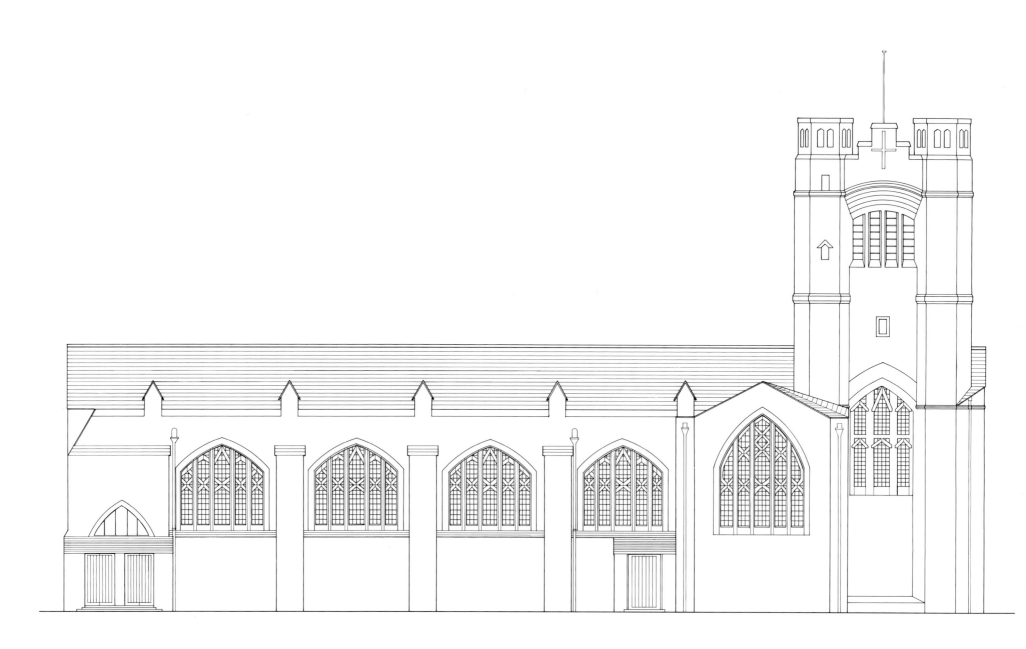

0   5m

0   15ft

End elevations

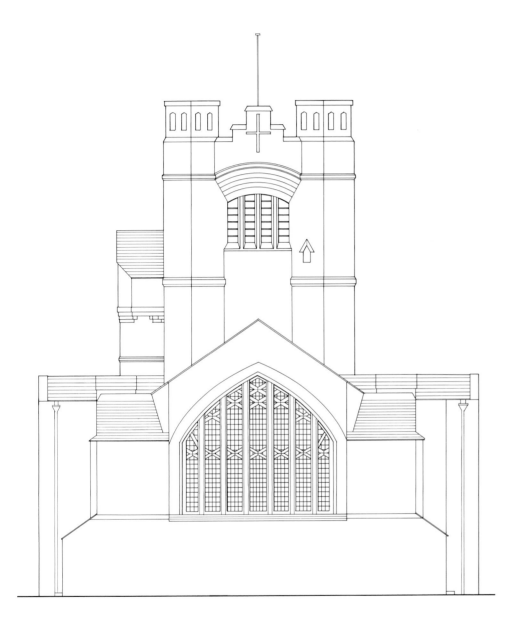

West elevation

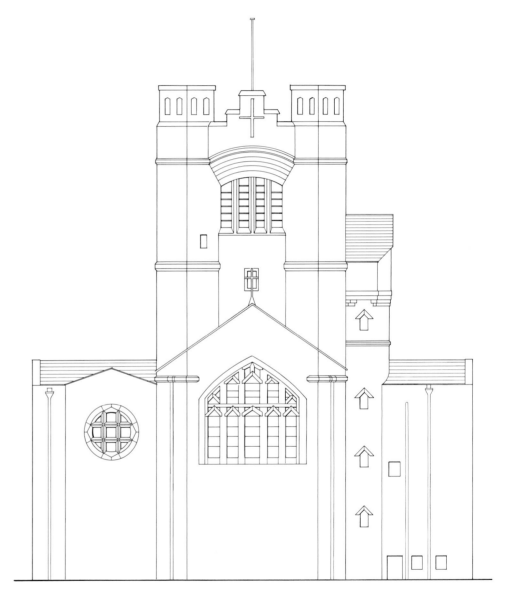

East elevation

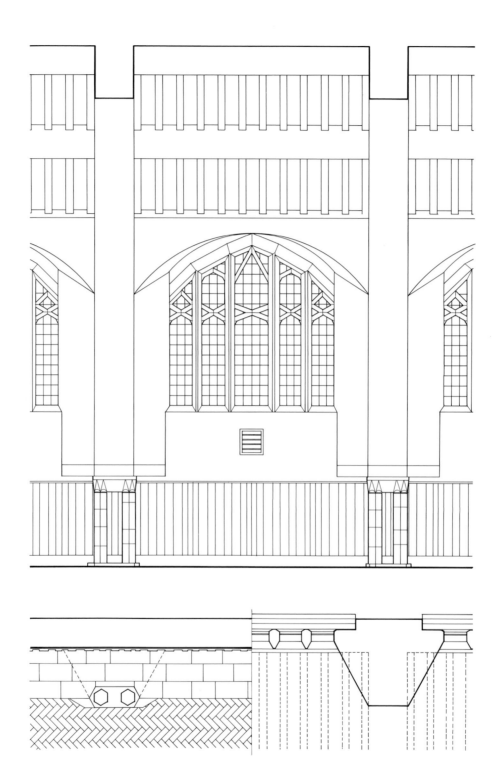

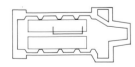

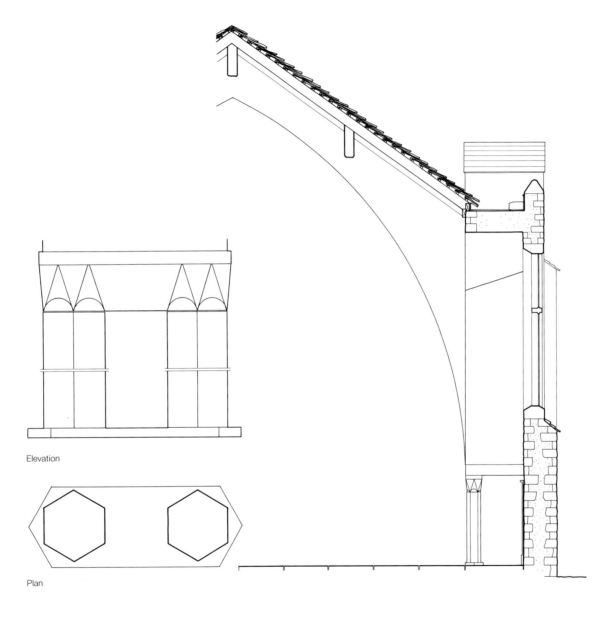

0 ⊢ 300mm

0 ⊢ 1ft

Elevation

Plan

Column details

Section through nave facing east

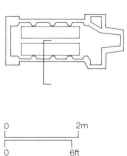

0 ⊢ 2m

0 ⊢ 6ft

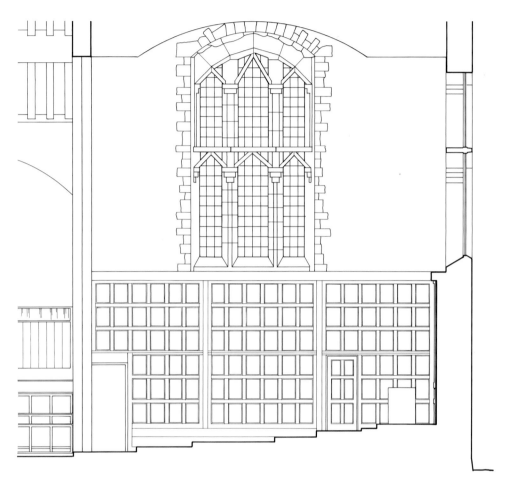

Elevation of chancel

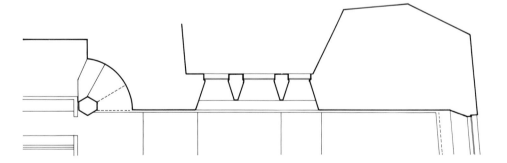

Plan of chancel

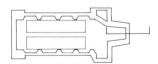

Detail of choir stalls

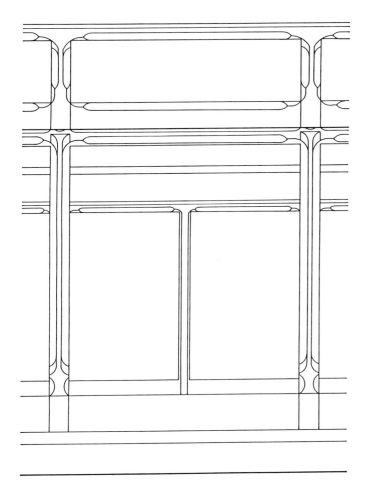

Elevation to typical bay

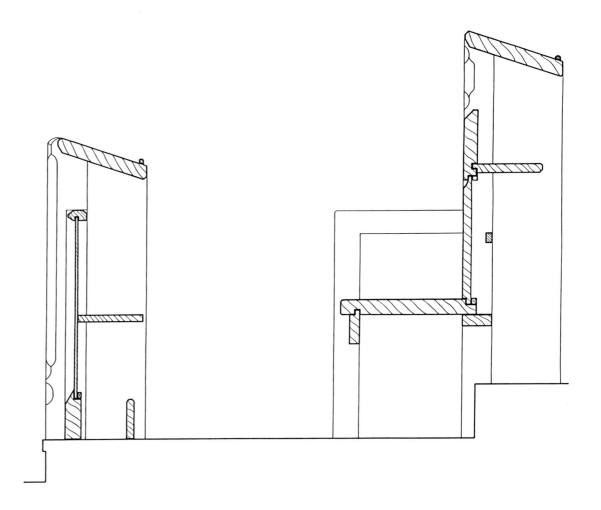

Cross section through choir stalls

0   200mm

0   6in

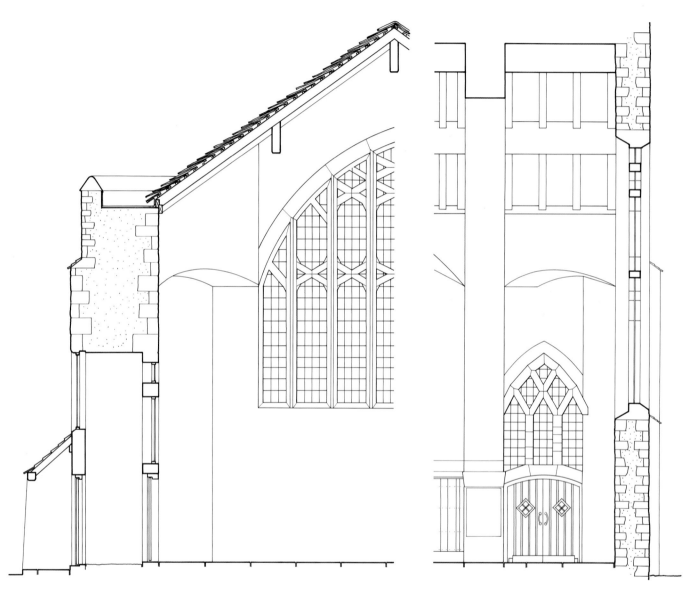

Section through south entrance   Internal elevation to south entrance

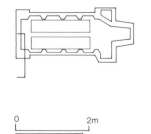

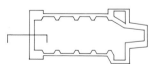

0   2m

0   6ft

Internal elevation to south entrance doors

0   200mm

0   6in

Author's acknowledgements

I would like to thank the Reverend Michael Berk and Mark Worthington the Curate of St Andrew's for the assistance and courtesy extended on my several visits to the church. Thanks also to the staff of the Durham County Records Office and the RIBA Drawings Collection who helped with the research. I am particularly grateful to Martin Charles, not only for the photographs, but for some provocative insights that aided the enquiry. Kingston University supported the research by assisting with travel costs. Finally thanks to Margy for patiently typing the several drafts.

Illustration acknowledgements

Black and white referential illustrations have been provided courtesy of the following: British Architectural Library, RIBA, London: figs 3, 9, 10, 26, 29, 39, and back cover; Martin Charles: figs 1, 15, 16, 23, 24, 30, 32, 38, 40, 41, 43–51; © Country Life Picture Library: fig 33; RCHME © Crown Copyright: figs 35–37.

Chronology

1852 Edward Schroeder Prior born 4 June.

1855 Father dies in a riding accident.

1856 Mother moves the family to Harrow where Prior will attend school.

1870 Enters Gonville and Caius College, Cambridge.

1872 Represents Cambridge in High Jump, Long Jump and Hurdles against Oxford, and wins the British Amateur High Jump.

1874 Articled to Norman Shaw.

1877 Begins his stint as Clerk of Works on Shaw's St Margaret's, Ilkley. Study tour of Belgium with Ernest Newton. Morris & Co opens showroom in Oxford Street. Morris gives his first public lecture on 'The Decorative Arts'.

1879 Begins his own practice with a setting-up commission from Shaw of Carr Manor, near Leeds. A series of buildings in and around Harrow and Bridport formed the basis of his practice.

1882 Morris's first collection of essays 'Hope and Fears for Art' published.

1884 Founding member of the Art Workers' Guild. 11 August marries Louise Isabella, second daughter of the Rev F W Maunsell of Symondsbury, Dorset. The couple were to have two daughters. Prior designed with William Lethaby a memorial window for St John the Baptist Church where he was married. Commission for Holy Trinity, Bothenhampton, Quay Terrace, Bridport.

1885 Design for Henry Martyn Hall, Cambridge.

1887 Elected Fellow of the RIBA, proposed by E J May, J Belcher and A Blomfield.

1888 First Arts and Crafts Exhibition Societies public show.

1889 Delivers his first public lecture entitled 'Texture as a Condition of Art and a Necessity for Architecture' to the Edinburgh Congress of National Association for the Advancement of Art in Relation to Industry. Morris was in the Chair. Begins to produce 'Prior's Early English Glass'.

1890 Designs the Harrow Music School building.

1891 Designs Pembroke College Mission in Walworth. Architects' Registration Bill put before Parliament.

1892 Prior contributes an article entitled 'The Profession and its Ghosts' to the collection 'Architecture: a Profession or an Art?' edited by Shaw and T G Jackson. He resigns from the RIBA in protest against its examination policy.

1894 Moves to 10 Melina Place, St John's Wood. Voysey lives next door and probably influences his design for the swimming baths at Bridport.

1895 Exhibits wax model of a radical house at the Royal Academy.

1896 Design for The Barn, Exmouth. He lives close by for long periods to supervise the construction. Morris dies.

1900 His first book, 'The History of Gothic Art in England', is published.

1901 He is appointed to the editorial board of the *Architectural Review*. He contributes a series of articles thereafter.

1902 Secretary of the Arts and Crafts Exhibitions Society.

1903 Design for Kelling Place (later Home Place), Holt, Norfolk. A Randall Wells acts as site architect. Roker and Fulwell New Church Committee formed in October. John Priestman, a local shipbuilder, donates £6,000 towards the new church.

1904 Design for Medical Schools, Cambridge. The Bishop of Durham consents to the division of the parish of Monkwearmouth and Prior gives estimate of £9,980 to build St Andrew's.

1905 Priestman chairs a new informal committee to oversee the final stages of design. Prior's estimate set of drawings are dated May.

1906 Randall Wells sets out St Andrew's in January and remains living close by to supervise work throughout. Ecclesiastical Commissioners approve the church but with reservations concerning the unusual column arrangements. Foundation stone laid by Mrs Priestman on 12 June. Prior is Master of the Art Workers' Guild.

1907 Randall Wells's reply to the Commissioners concerns in January suggest that walls are constructed. The church is consecrated on 19 July. The total cost of the church is £13,117, the fabric costing £7,881-8-4, furnishings £5,255-11-8.

1912 Appointed Slade Professor of Architectural History at Cambridge. Publishes 'An Account of Medieval Figure Sculpture in England'.

1913 Designs St Edmund's Church, Parkstone, Dorset, with Arthur Grove.

1922 Publishes 'Eight Chapters on English Medieval Art'.

1927 Produces design for the chancel of St Andrew's, executed by MacDonald Gill.

1932 Prior dies on 19 August. He was buried in an unmarked grave at St Mary's, Apuldram.

Select Bibliography

Addleshaw G and F Etchells, *The Architectural Setting of Anglican Worship* (Faber & Faber: London, 1948). Subtitled 'An Inquiry into the arrangements for Public Worship in the Church of England from the Reformation to the present day', this is a good survey resulting from the collaboration of canon and architect.

Comito M, *Gimson and the Barnsleys* (Evan Bros Ltd: London, 1980). This is the only book-length treatment of these important furniture designers and architects who took Morris's call to the crafts most to heart.

Davey P, *Arts and Crafts Architecture* (Phaidon: London, 1994). A well illustrated, extensive and witty survey of the work of all its leading proponents.

Goodhart-Rendell H, *English Architecture since the Regency* (Constable & Co: London, 1953). First delivered as the Slade Lectures, this remains one of the best general guides to Victorian Architecture, delivered with the passion of a late participant.

Hoare G, and G Pyne, *Prior's Barn and Gimson's Coxen; Two Arts & Crafts Houses* (privately published from 'Selforth', Little Knowle, Budleigh Salterton, 1978). A detailed account of Prior's first radical building, drawing upon the knowledge of local historians.

Lambourne L, *Utopian Craftsmen* (Astragal Books: London, 1980). Although Prior is only mentioned in passing this book is one of the best general surveys of the Arts and Crafts movement well capturing its spirit and philosophy.

Lethaby W, *Philip Webb and his Work* (Raven Oak Press: London, 1979). This is probably the best book of Lethaby's many to understand the architectural source of Prior's inspiration, in particular the chapter entitled 'Some architects of the 19th Century and Two Ways of building'.

Massé H, *The Art Workers' Guild, 1884–1934* (Shakespeare Head Press: Oxford, 1935). This definitive account of the Guild which became the principal forum of the Arts and Crafts movement, includes a chapter on its origins written by Prior.

Morris W, *Architecture, Industry and Wealth* (Longmans, Green & Co: London, 1902). This collection of his essays is to be recommended for its concentration upon architecture.

Pevsner N, *Some Architectural Writers of the Nineteenth Century*, (Clarendon Press: Oxford, 1972). Good accounts of all the noteworthy writers provide an essential picture of the background to Prior's thinking about architecture. Kerr's essay 'English Architecture Thirty Years Hence' and Morris's 'The Revival of Architecture' are reprinted as Appendices.

Prior E S, *The Cathedral Builders of England* (Seeley & Co: London, 1905).

Prior E S, *Eight Chapters on English Medieval Architecture*, (Cambridge University Press, 1922).

Prior E S, *A History of Gothic Art in England* (George Bell and Sons: London, 1900).

Prior E S, *Medieval Figure Sculpture in England* (Cambridge University Press, 1912). All four of Prior's books, as the titles indicate, dealt with his favourite architecture from slightly different viewpoints. Like his friend Lethaby, he dug into the Cathedral building rolls to glean information on medieval masons to supplement his vast first-hand experience of the buildings.

Ruskin J, *Lectures on Art and Architecture* (George Routledge & Son: London, 1854). The Edinburgh Lectures make a good introduction to Ruskin's thoughts on architecture for he presented them as a summary of his earlier *Seven Lamps of Architecture* and *The Stones of Venice*.

Saint A, *Richard Norman Shaw* (Yale University Press: New Haven and London, 1976). The definitive and a model biography of this great Victorian architect includes a good chapter on the office as it was when Prior was a pupil of Shaw.

Service A, *Edwardian Architecture* (Thames and Hudson: London, 1977). A successful summary of the material collected in a book of essays he edited earlier, *Edwardian Architecture and its Origins* (Architectural Press: London, 1975) which includes a short pioneering study of Prior's work by Christopher Grillet.

Summerson J, *The Turn of the Century; Architecture in Britain around 1900* (University of Glasgow Press, 1976). Originally delivered as the W A Cagill Memorial Lecture, this makes a good introduction to the period, for it sketches a picture of the events, mood and all the important architects working around 1900 delivered with the author's inimitable wit and breadth.

Notes

1 *St Andrew's Vestry Records Book*. Annual Parochial Church Meeting, 22 April 1927, Durham County Archives, EP/Mo SA 6/1.

2 E S Prior, 'The New Cathedral for Liverpool', *Architectural Review*, 1901 (vol 10), p144.

3 N Pevsner, *The Buildings of England; Northumberland* (Penguin Books: London, 1953), p469.

4 Some biographical information on Prior can be found in the RIBA Library but the details here are drawn from the unpublished PhD of Lynne Walker, *E S Prior 1852–1932*, Birkbeck College, University of London, 1978.

5 A Saint, *Richard Norman Shaw* (Yale University Press: New Haven and London, 1976), p130. See pp185–91 for details of Shaw's pupils and assistants.

6 Walker, *op cit*, pp81–2.

7 Saint, *op cit*, pp295 and 417.

8 H Goodhart-Rendell, 'Rogue Architects of the Victorian Age', *RIBA Journal*, April 1949 (vol 56), p257.

9 Saint, *op cit*, p186. This comment was ascribed to Shaw by his son Robert Shaw in manuscript notes on his father.

10 Obituaries appeared in *The Architect*, 26 August 1932, p236, *RIBA Journal*, 15 October 1932, pp858–9, and *The Builder*, 26 August 1932, p328.

11 Walker, *op cit*, p104. Prior's client was Thomas Allbutt, an enlightened medical practitioner whom George Eliot used as model for Tertius Lydgate in *Middlemarch*.

12 Saint, *op cit*, p406.

13 Walker, *op cit*, pp313–49. Holy Trinity was largely paid for by J Gundy, Chairman of the West Bay Building Company.

14 H Massé, *The Art Workers' Guild, 1884–1934* (Shakespeare Head Press: Oxford, 1935), p7.

15 *ibid*.

16 R Kerr, 'English Architecture Thirty Years Hence' in N Pevsner, *Some Architectural Thinkers of the 19th Century* (Clarendon Press: Oxford, 1972), pp309–10.

17 J Ruskin, *Lectures on Arts and Architecture* (George Routledge & Son: London, 1854), p111.

18 E S Prior, *The Origins of the Guild*, in Massé, *op cit*, p8.

19 *Ibid*, p11.

20 *Ibid*, p12.

21 May Morris, *The Introductions to the Collected Works of William Morris*, vol 2 (Oriole Editions: New York, 1973), p460. The Arts and Crafts Exhibition Society was formed to publicize the work of AWG members which its own constitution forbade. Morris was on the selection committee for the first show. He proposed the formation of the NAAA in September 1888. E Lemire, *The Unpublished Lectures of William Morris* (Wayne State University Press: Detroit, 1969), p272.

22 Lemire, *op cit*, p280; and *Transactions of the National Association for the Advancement of Art*, 1890, p332. In the discussion that followed Prior's paper he disagreed with Morris's contention that there could never be an iron architecture.

23 E S Prior, 'Texture as a Quality of Art and a Condition for Architecture', *Transactions*, *op cit*, p319.

24 *Ibid*, p319–21.

25 *Ibid*, p320.

26 *Ibid*, pp322–3.

27 *Ibid*, p322.

28 W Morris, 'The Revival of Architecture' in *Architecture, Industry and Wealth* (Longmans, Green & Co: London, 1902), p198.

29 Wordsworth and Coleridge, *The Lyrical Ballads*, eds R Brett and A Jones, (Methuen & Co Ltd: London, 1963), pp261 and 244.

30 S T Coleridge, *Biographia Literaria* (Dent & Son: London, 1965), p167.

31 W Morris, 'The Influence of Building Materials upon Architecture' in *Architecture, Industry and Wealth*, *op cit*, p250.

32 See T Garnham, *The Oxford Museum* (Phaidon: London, 1992), for a discussion of this.

33 Prior, *op cit*, p322.

34 *Ibid*.

35 *Ibid*.

36 Jacquetta Hawkes in her book *A Land* (The Cresset Press: London, 1951), explores the conundrum of where one draws the line between us and nature, given the theory of evolution; the monkey, the mollusc, microbes, or the rocks laid down from primeval mud?

37 Prior, *op cit*, p322.

38 *Ibid*, p329.

39 E S Prior, 'Architectural Modelling' in *The Builder*, 29 June 1895 (vol 68) p483.

40 *Ibid*. Up to Soane's time models were commonly used, but Prior's was only the second model at the RA in 20 years.

41 The client for The Barn, W H Weatherhall, was an old Harrovian. G Hoare and G Pyne, *Prior's Barn and Gimson's Coxen; Two Arts and Crafts Houses* (privately published with unnumbered pages).

42 Prior read Viollet-le-Duc's *Discourse* published in 1889 in which he illustrates an X-plan town house.

43 Prior was a keen butterfly collector.

44 *Architectural Review*, 1906 (vol 19) p70.

45 H M Taylor and Joan Taylor, *Anglo-Saxon Architecture* (Cambridge University Press, 1965), p338. Bishop Biscop brought John the archchanter to teach the Gregorian chant which was first sung in these islands at St Peter's. Bede also had an association with this monastic settlement.

46 St Peter's, Monkwearmouth is mentioned for its western porch in Prior's *A History of Gothic Art in England* (George Bell & Sons, London, 1900), p48.

47 Copy Letter book relating to the building of the new church, 19 October 1903. Durham County Records. EP/Mo SA/1.

48 *Ibid*. Letter to S O Austen, 30 December 1903.

49 Priestman & Co, established in 1882, was a typical late nineteenth-century shipyard that grew from little more than a one-man workshop to become a large, industrial concern. This was the dawn of iron steamers, Priestman & Co specializing in the design and construction of tramp steamers. It is estimated that he donated more than £½ million to charitable concerns during his lifetime and he left £1,504,744 at his death. He received a knighthood in 1913 and a Baronetcy in 1934 in recognition of his public works.

50 Letter from Chairman of the Roker and Fulwell New Church Committee to Priestman, 20 April 1904. Durham County Archives, EP/Mo SA/1.

51 Charles Prior was son-in-law of BF Westcott, the previous Bishop who had died in 1901. He was also a close friend of the vicar of All Saints, Monkwearmouth, the Rev D S Bontflower, a former student of Caius. Walker, *op cit*, p473.

52 This information is given in a summary of events pertaining to the commission and building of St Andrew's, drawn up as a result of a dispute between Priestman and church wardens. It seems that Priestman lent £1,206 in 1909 and that the church wardens were unable or reluctant to repay. In January 1910 Priestman wrote to the Chairman that he 'never though [he] would behave in such a contemptible way'. Durham County Archives EP/Mo SA4/3.

53 Lethaby had introduced a 'School of Handicraft and Design' to the Architectural Association where he prompted his radical views. In a talk to the School Prior said: '… that he belonged to the same school of architectural thought as Mr Lethaby, … the school which believed that architecture was rational building'. *AA Notes*, November 1896, Vol II, p120. See T Garnham, 'William Lethaby and the Two Ways of Building', *AA Files*, No 10, Autumn 1985, pp27–43 for discussion of this.

54 E S Prior, 'Church building as it is and how it might be', *Architectural Review*, 1898, p157.

55 E S Prior, *The New Cathedral for Liverpool*, *op cit*, pp145–6.

56 J Davies (ed), *A New Dictionary of Liturgy and Worship* (SCM Press Ltd: London, 1986), p 3. See also G Addleshaw & and F Etchells, *The Architectural Setting of Anglican Worship*, (Faber & Fabe: London, 1948).

57 E S Prior, 'Art Study at Cambridge', *RIBA Journal*, 29 June 1912, p594.

58 Rev D Marsh, *Description and Notes concerning the Church of St Andrew's, Roker*, p27. Prior described Fulwell as 'A quarry of beautiful limestone … [but] the craft of using it in building had died out.' *The Builder*, 12 October 1907 (vol 93) p386.

59 A Randall Wells, Letter to the Ecclesiastical Commissioners, 3 January 1907. Durham County Archives EP/Mo SA 4/56 (1).

60 Letter from Ecclesiastical Commissioners, 21 February 1906, Durham County Archives EP/Mo SA/55(1).

61 Prior, *A History of Gothic Art in England*, *op cit*, pp46–9.

62 W R Lethaby, *The Church of Sancta Sophia* (Macmillan & Co: London, 1894), p247.

63 Randall Wells, *op cit*.

64 Randall Wells, *The Builder*, 7 November 1907 (vol 93) p563.

65 Marsh, *op cit*, pp17–18.

66 RIBA Drawings Collection, RAN 5/H/4 1–15.

67 Ironically Shaw was on the panel that rejected Prior's design on 1 December 1886. In November a panel containing J D Sedding and James Brook said that: 'The character of the roofing proposed is extraordinary, expensive and unsafe, and not to be recommended according to construction and decor, though the idea is a suggestive one.' Walker, *op cit*, pp330–31.

68 Prior, letter to *The Builder*, 23 November 1907, pp562–3.

69 Wells, *op cit*.

70 The Congress was extensively reported in the Journal of the RIBA, 25 August 1906 (vol XIII). Otto Wagner attended. Prior was Master of the AWG in this year and chaired a conference on William Morris held to coincide with the Congress. See Massé, *op cit*, pp113–14.

71 Prior described the Gothic of the Ile de France as 'Chairworks of articulated stone pegged to the ground by pinnacles', *A History of Gothic Art*, *op cit*, p9. But he disagreed with Lethaby's view that all European Gothic was in some way the offspring of this 'Mother' art.

72 Prior, *Eight Chapters on Medieval Art* (Cambridge University Press, 1922), p1.

73 Taylor and Taylor, *op cit*.

74 Prior, *The New Cathedral for Liverpool*, p143.

75 Prior, *Eight Chapters on English Medieval Art*, *op cit*, p9.

76 Prior had worked on restorations at Kelsale and Framlingham in Suffolk. He mentions Blythburgh, a particularly fine example of this type in his *Cathedral Builders of England*, (Seeley & Co: London, 1905), p94.

77 Marsh, *op cit*, p2.

78 Saint, *op cit*, pp276–93.

79 Prior, *Eight Chapters on English Medieval Art*, *op cit*, p131.

80 Prior, *A History of Gothic Art in England*, *op cit*, pp428 and 447–8.

81 Semper was in England helping to prepare the Great Exhibition. There is a manuscript – 'Practical Art in Metals, its Technology, History and Styles' – at the Victoria and Albert Museum (MS 86 ff 64) where his early thoughts that lead to his monumental *Der Stil* could have been read by Prior's circle.

82 Gimson had met Morris when he was only 19 and had been given an introduction to the office of J D Sedding by him. M Comito, *Gimson and the Barnsleys* (Evans Bros Ltd: London, 1980), pp13–15. The following account is drawn from this book; see in particular pp102–6.

83 This account of the church furnishing draws extensively upon the Rev Marsh's description.

84 Marsh, *op cit*, p15.

85 *Ibid*, p11.

86 Prior's specification cited in Walker, *op cit*, p384. This technique would produce glass only up to 8 x 6 in. Christopher Whall used Prior's glass.

87 Marsh, *op cit*, p18.

88 *Ibid*.

89 *Ibid*, p29.

90 *Ibid*, p11.

91 *Ibid*.

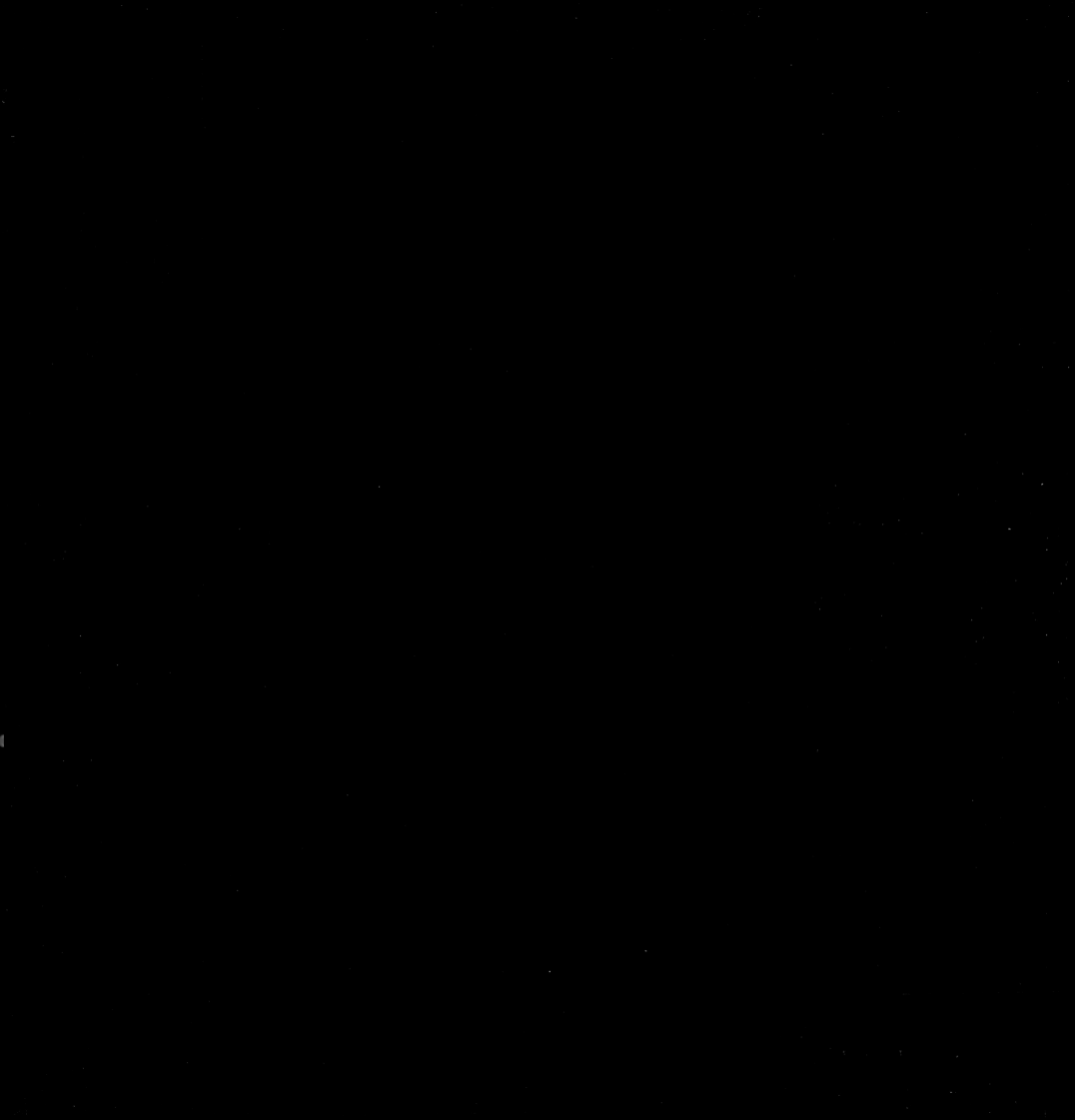

Charles Rennie Mackintosh
Glasgow School of Art
Glasgow, Scotland 1897–1909

James Macaulay

Photography
Mark Fiennes; cover detail
also by Mark Fiennes
Drawings
Paul Clarke

1

When Charles Rennie Mackintosh (1868–1928) first enrolled as a part-time evening student in 1883 at the Glasgow School of Art he began an association with the school which lasted almost until his departure from Glasgow thirty years later.

In the 1880s the school of art was housed in a corner of the MacLellan Galleries erected in 1855 to accommodate the city's art collection. The juxtaposition, however, was uncomfortable and there were frequent complaints about the inadequacy of the space allotted for the art classes. A report from the examiner of the Science and Art Department at South Kensington, which oversaw art education, stated that the rooms were 'ill adapted for the purposes of a school of art… with the aggravation of the grey dull atmosphere prevailing here for half the year the students labour under positive disadvantage'. The modelling and lecture rooms, reached at the top of the building after a climb of seventy-two steps, were cold in winter but without heat because of the fire danger from the timber linings and so hot in the summer that lectures had to be abandoned in April.[1]

Despite these drawbacks the reputation of the Glasgow School was high. In the league table of schools administered by the Science and Art Department, 'in the National Awards Glasgow stood third highest among the art schools of the kingdom in the number of medals and prizes'.[2] Thus, in 1892 in the National Competition Prizes the school's governors could record with some satisfaction: 'Gold Medal, for the 5th year in succession, taken this year by Chas R. McIntosh for Architecture'.[3] Indeed, as the *Glasgow Herald* noted some months later, it was 'the first obtained in Scotland for architecture'.[4] Mackintosh's entry was a heavily classical chapter-house, in the mode

of the Leeds Town Hall, which he had submitted earlier that same year for another competition.[5]

In the spring of 1885 the head of the art school resigned 'only in consequence of the apathy that is shown towards the institution'.[6] His successor was made of sterner stuff. He was Francis Newbery (1855–1946), the most celebrated of all the heads of the Glasgow School of Art, who, having been selected from a shortlist of three, was appointed in May at a salary of £500 a year.[7] Having taught at South Kensington, Newbery had metropolitan standards which he introduced at Glasgow without, it seems, arousing antagonism unlike others in more recent times from south of the border. In his inaugural address to the students at the beginning of the new session he announced that a committee of local architects, which would include such eminent practitioners as William Leiper, J.J. Burnet and H.E. Clifford, would oversee architectural education in the school. He also 'stated the position taken up by the school upon design… to practically supply that which Glasgow at present needs – namely a race of designers for her own creation'.[8]

Before the end of the year not only was 'an allowance of 7/6 a week granted for a lad to assist the janitor as messenger and jobbing hand and librarian' but Newbery had offered 'to give a short course of public lectures on art and suggests that entry money should form a nucleus of a fund for a new school of art'.[9] He even managed to persuade the governors before his first year in Glasgow was up to readjust the staff salaries 'owing to the necessity for raising the standard of work in the school'.[10] New classes were introduced and in 1895 it was agreed to pay 'Miss Helen Walton for China Class 20 weeks…£7:10:0.

1 Charles Rennie Mackintosh, in a photograph taken in 1903 at the age of 35.
2, 3 Pages from Mackintosh's architectural notebooks showing details of iron railings at Chipping Camden Church, **2**, and decorative leadwork at Campden House, **3**, undated.

4 Flower study by Mackintosh; Veronica, pencil and watercolour, dated 1915.
5, 6 Watercolours by Mackintosh: The Village of La Lagonne, **5**, and Port Vendres, **6**, painted after 1923.
7 One of Mackintosh's sketches of Newton Castle, Blairgowrie made in 1909.

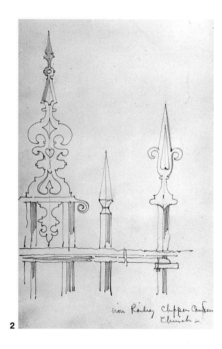

2

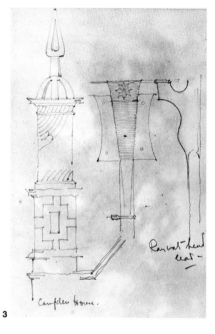

3

Mrs Newbery… £10:10:0 for Design Instruction in Needlework Class'.[11] Newbery also made use of his southern contacts to invite to the school such eminent designers as Walter Crane 'when a conversazione might be held' who returned two years later in 1888 to lecture on 'Expression and Imitation in Art' and William Morris who in 1889 spoke, inevitably, on 'Arts and Crafts' having intimated that he 'would try for once to eschew politics; and that all the more as I see something hopeful in the line that Crane and others are on; in a small way I mean'.[12]

Contact with ideas furth of Scotland was also gained through the burgeoning periodicals. For architects *The Builder* was essential reading, as was *Academy Architecture* in which very soon many of Mackintosh's early works would be illustrated. More influential, innovative and broadly based was *The Studio* begun in 1893; it was obviously scrutinized by Mackintosh and other members of The Four, some of whose works were illustrated in *The Studio* as early as 1897.

The Four were Charles Rennie Mackintosh, **1**, Herbert McNair (1868–1955) and the two sisters Margaret (1865–1933) and Frances Macdonald (1873–1921). It seems that the two men were introduced to the sisters, who were full-time students at the school of art, by Newbery and in 1899 Herbert McNair married Frances, an example followed a year later by Mackintosh and Margaret Macdonald.

The artistic collaboration among The Four was such that their products in furniture, metalwork and in paintings are at first glance almost indistinguishable from one another although as Muthesius noted: 'Mackintosh's architectonic sensibility brings to the group's creations those strict tectonic foundations that are apparent

despite all their imaginative qualities'.[13] Thus, while Mackintosh indulged in an early experimental phase of using abstract symbolism and attenuated human figures in watercolour paintings, his main interest developed around architecture. Not only did that demand a more rigorous and cerebral approach to design but it gave his work a spatial dimension on a large scale, all of which led to a continual artistic maturing which did not happen with the other members of The Four.

Mackintosh's architectural notebooks, **2**, **3**, which survive from 1874 to 1921, are full of architectural jottings, many of which found their way into his built works. Yet, he never abandoned his interest in painting even if in a busy professional life it was sometimes only in the holidays that there was time for him to work on the flower studies, **4**. However, during the years of enforced idleness in southern France Mackintosh's watercolours assume a magisterial authority over the Mediterranean forms which he was no longer creating in three dimensions, **5**, **6**.

Mackintosh's early career

Mackintosh had begun his architectural career in 1884 with an apprenticeship. On its conclusion five years later he moved to the office of Honeyman and Keppie (one of the most prestigious in the city) where a fellow draughtsman was Herbert McNair. Another member of the firm was Alexander McGibbon who was invited by Newbery in 1890 'to act as Visiting Master to the architectural class' of the school of art.[14] McNair too left the firm, setting up his own

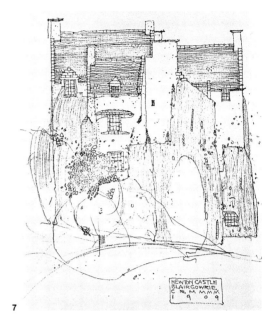

7

4

5

6

10

design studio in Glasgow before he and Frances went to Liverpool. After their return to Glasgow in 1909 they both taught in the school of art.[15]

When Mackintosh entered the firm of Honeyman and Keppie, John Honeyman (1831–1914) had been a practising architect for almost three decades, although with the onset of blindness he would retire in 1904. Honeyman had originally been destined for the church, a connection which would have helped in securing the many church commissions in later years beginning in 1862 with Lansdowne Church, Great Western Road, Glasgow which has justly been described as 'perhaps the most attractive Victorian Gothic church in the city'.[16] Its Early English style owes little, however, to the medieval cathedral which later interested Honeyman scholastically and on which he carried out restoration work.[17]

Mackintosh was brought up in Dennistoun, a residential suburb immediately to the east of the cathedral which, until George Gilbert Scott's new university was underway, was the city's largest building. Not surprisingly the cathedral was an attraction to Mackintosh who drew its graveyard monuments; his first large watercolour in 1890, perhaps inspired by his new association with Honeyman, was of the mighty double-storied eastern arm of the thirteenth century building as viewed against a setting sun.[18]

Not only was Honeyman a learned and cultured man who well understood the inheritance of Scottish architecture, as witnessed by restorations at Iona Abbey (1891) and Brechin Cathedral (1904), but he was well versed in contemporary architectural theory as demonstrated in the daring boldness of the Ca d'Oro (1872), **8**. Commissioned as

a furniture warehouse, it has a stone arcade with a stone and iron superstructure where a combination of Gothic tracery and decoration shows an adept awareness and intelligent application of John Ruskin's theories from *The Stones of Venice*. Such structural rationalism, perhaps to be expected in a place as technologically innovative as Glasgow, is also found in the *oeuvre* of Alexander 'Greek' Thomson who designed the cast iron Buck's Head building (1863) as well as the trio of neo-classical churches which give his architecture a European importance. The only one to survive intact is the St Vincent Street Church (1857–59), **9**, where a vast temple-like interior of rosy hue has an enveloping gallery carried on cast-iron columns, their colouring inspired perhaps by Owen Jones, and all resting on a basement gouged out of the side of a hill.

Although one does not know how the office of Honeyman and Keppie was structured it would seem, given the age of Honeyman and the limited artistic inclination of Keppie, that the partners handed a brief to Mackintosh who was allowed to evolve the design concept and then work up the details so that he soon began to develop a personal style.

At first glance Queen's Cross Church (1897) looks like many another Gothic rendering in its free style, **10**, and in the box plan containing a chancel and galleries; nevertheless, the spatial disturbances in the disposition of the architectural elements are almost Mannerist as is also the weird avian decoration of the pulpit. Unlike the Old Testament declamations of Thomson's churches, Mackintosh imbues his church with a spirituality which harkens to the wooded groves of pagan worship.

8 The Ca d'Oro, Glasgow, completed by John Honeyman in 1872.
9 St Vincent Street Church, 1857–59, designed by Alexander 'Greek' Thomson.
10 Mackintosh, perspective rendering of Saint Matthew's Church, now Queen's Cross Church, Glasgow, 1897.
11 Pencil, ink and colour wash drawing of the Glasgow School of Art showing the elevations to Scott Street and Dalhousie Street; prepared by Mackintosh in 1910.

8

9

The Glasgow School of Art

In 1882 a proposal had been put forward by the city's Lord Provost for a museum, art gallery and school of art to be constructed on the vacant plot adjoining the Corporation Galleries; although sketch plans were exhibited at the end of the year nothing happened.[19] Yet the idea did not die and when it was revived at the end of the decade a scheme was prepared for Honeyman and Keppie by the new draughtsman.[20] Mackintosh's scheme in its broad layout and general massing is a further reminder of the Leeds Town Hall but overlaid with Thomson detailing, which is hardly surprising given that Keppie had worked with James Sellars who had been Thomson's draughtsman. Then in March 1894 the art school's governors made an application to the Bellahouston Trust for a grant for a purpose-built school of art. Two of the architect governors, W. Forrest Salmon and J.J. Burnet, together with Newbery were asked to measure the floor area of the existing spaces and then to 'compute what would be sufficient space for the accommodation of a complete school in a new building'.

A month later William Leiper was added to the sub-committee. Although it reported to the governing board in May six months passed before the Bellahouston trustees asked 'if you could ascertain more definitely as to the cost of the site referred to'. Early in the new year of 1895 the trustees gave their decision. They 'could not see their way to go beyond the sum of £10,000 to be made up of the site purchase for £6,000, to be gifted once the school had raised a similar sum, plus £4,000 in cash'. Thereafter events moved fairly rapidly and by the autumn of that year the trustees had secured the ground in Renfrew Street.

In the following spring Newbery was 'asked to prepare a block plan showing how the whole site might be utilized' with room dimensions and window sizes 'and how much of this accommodation might be immediately constructed. Such information would enable a building committee to frame conditions for a competition'.[21] At first only eight local firms were invited to compete but soon four others were added to the list. Each was supplied with a printed set of conditions which was the design brief. Competitors were required to submit 'a plan of each floor, a longitudinal section, two cross sections, and three elevations, north, east and south'. The elevations were to be in outline only without any shading or etching and no perspectives were to be allowed. The south elevation 'may not have any lights in its walls' (because of adjoining buildings) …except perhaps in the upper floor which would contain the Director's room, 'in a central position', with his studio on the north side where the spaces 'should be, as far as possible, rigidly kept for class-rooms' with the windows 'free from mullions and small panes, and should be in the length of the room'. It was also required that, 'The school museum need not be a special room, but might be a feature in connection with the staircase'. Provision was to be made for a library, two lecture theatres and the studios would include one for still life and flower painting with 'a conservatory, with an exposure to the sun, in which plants and flowers, when not in use, may be kept'.[22]

Having read the brief the competing architects, who included such well known local names as John A. Campbell, H. and D. Barclay and the Salmons, sent a roundrobin to the governors stating unequivocally that the proposed building could not be provided with the funds

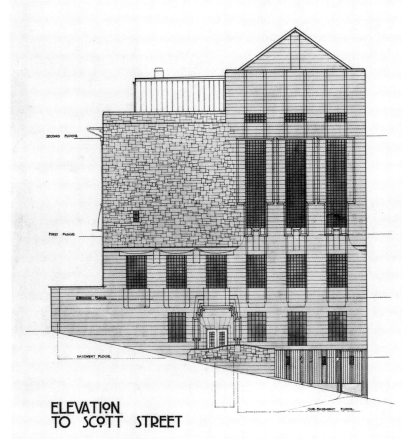

ELEVATION
TO SCOTT STREET

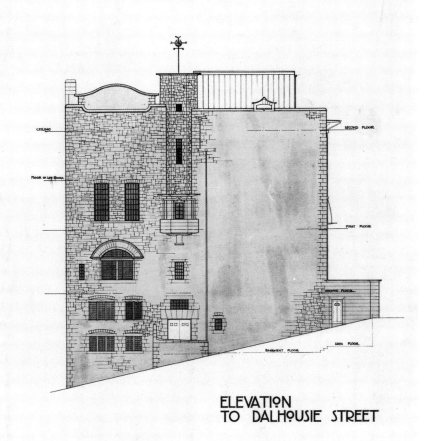

ELEVATION
TO DALHOUSIE STREET

12

available. After an exchange of correspondence the architects were asked to 'state what portion of their building could be carried out within the limit of £14,000'. Although the governors' viewpoint was that 'it is but a plain building that is required' they did agree eventually that the competitors could shade 'such portion of their design as can be carried out for the sum' while indicating the cost of the total building.

On the afternoon of Wednesday, 13 January 1897 the winning firm was announced as Honeyman and Keppie. According to local mythology Newbery, recognizing Mackintosh's hand in the firm's competition drawings, influenced the building committee's decision, **12**. The surviving records do not bear that out and, indeed, the information which Newbery collected for the brief was 'to be furnished only to the governors'.[23] None of the competition drawings have survived. The most complete surviving set are those which were prepared by Honeyman, Keppie and Mackintosh, 'in accordance with the terms of our appointment', once the school of art was finished.[24] These and some preparatory elevations show the maturing of Mackintosh's design since, for Mackintosh, the first preparatory design was but an entry into a revelatory domain of ordering and re-ordering so that it is not surprising that his commissions were consistently over the allotted budget.

A perusal of the drawings shows that Mackintosh adhered closely to the brief although in certain instances he did feel that it was necessary to make deviations as was explained in the 'Description and Schedule of Contents' which formed part of his competition submission. The 'Description', which was only discovered in the school archives in the summer of 1992, opens with the statement that in the design 'economy

has been kept pointedly in view' so that 'the useless expenditure of money on mere embellishments has played no part.

'The accommodation has been arranged as far as possible according to the sizes and position suggested in the conditions of competition' except that architecture was now to be housed in the basement in preference to the library which was transferred to the ground floor as being more accessible. The only additions were a students' common room and anatomical rooms as Newbery had introduced the study of anatomy. The 'Description' also recounts the materials to be used. The basement floors were to 'be asphalted and floored with narrow boarding. The upper floors to be constructed of wooden joists carried on rolled iron girders and covered with narrow flooring. The vestibule, the floor of which is concrete over the heating chamber will be laid with slabs of Arbroath pavement enriched with designs in coloured marbles as shown on plans. All finishings will be of yellow pine. The lintels of large windows will be of rolled iron cased in plaster. The astragals of large windows will be casements of rolled steel.'

Claims have been made for the uniqueness of the heating system installed in the school, but it is worth quoting the architect in 1897: 'The system of ventilating suggested on the plans is by drawing from the outer air by a Blackman or other fan, a current, which being cleansed by a washing screen, passes over a heating coil… This system is almost too well known to require advocacy and has been applied with success to many well known buildings in Glasgow'.[25]

Today, the art school, because of later and very unsympathetic (not to say antagonistic) neighbouring encroachments, has lost something

12 The Building Committee of the Glasgow School of Art, painted by the Director of the school, Francis Newbery, in 1914. Mackintosh stands on the left with the plans of the school in his hand. Newbery is seated on the extreme right. Standing second from right is J.J. Burnet.

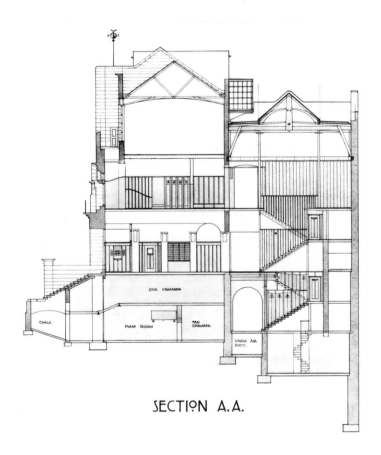

SECTION A.A.

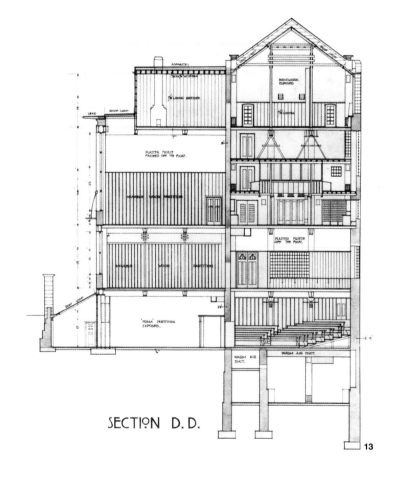

SECTION D.D.

13

of its significance as a Glasgow building. In the 1890s Glasgow was a city built of sandstone and the most common building type was the tenement, usually of three storeys with a dressed ashlar front with the cheaper rubble being used on the sides and rear. Turn of the century photographs, **14**, show how admirably the new school of art fitted into the urban pattern both in overall massing and height lines so that new as it was, stylistically it accorded beneficently with the local scene.

At the laying of the foundation stone in May 1898 John Honeyman and John Keppie were among the platform party; at the formal opening at the end of the next year the reply to the vote of thanks to the architects was given by Keppie. However, at the next annual public meeting of the school, Mackintosh was on the platform, although it seems that he had to listen to criticisms of the building which, when the sums were complete, cost a third more than the estimate of £14,000.[26]

It says much for the governors therefore, that when they came to consider the building of phase two early in 1907 they were prepared to continue with Honeyman and Keppie, where Mackintosh had been a partner since 1904, but on the condition that the architects were 'not at liberty to instruct any extra work or any alterations on the plans or specifications'. That was part of a memorandum devised by J.J. Burnet 'to meet the difficulties' of the building committee.[27] Even so, when Mackintosh was asked only a few weeks later for a complete set of drawings his response, though interesting, could not have cheered his clients. 'We think it undesirable to commit ourselves to any elevational treatment until the general scheme of internal arrangement is approved by the sub-committee'.[28]

The building and its sources

Increasingly, scholars have demonstrated how Mackintosh made use of his own sketches of buildings and of ornamental details in his own corpus of design, for Mackintosh was as eclectic as the next architect, the difference being that neither contemporary nor classical architecture features in his notebooks. Essentially, his interests were Decorated and Perpendicular churches and the domestic vernacular architecture of the later Tudor period; in Scotland it was the sculptural forms of the native tower-houses which he sought and recorded. Thus the starting point for the composition of the east elevation of the art school is a Mackintosh sketch of Maybole Castle, Ayrshire which he drew in 1895, **15**. Maybole Castle would have appealed to Mackintosh who in a lecture in 1891 urged his audience to consider the merits of Scotland's native architecture: 'that it is an architectural style of the modern as distinguished from the ancient world… That it is pre-eminently the arch(itecture) of our own forefathers and of our own land' and he drew attention to 'the extraordinary facility of our style in decorating, constructing, and in converting structural and useful features into elements of beauty'.[29]

In Mackintosh's Maybole Castle sketch the distinguishing features are the nearly equal vertical divisions and the sense of organic growth so that the summit burgeons with decoration. Though both are replicated in Mackintosh's art school design there is no overt historicism for it is the spirit that imbues Mackintosh's design not the time-worn details. Indeed, there is an honesty in the composition which is almost painful to behold. By accepting that each internal volume should be read individually on the external face, so that the pair of tall

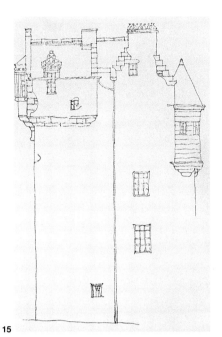

15

14

13 Pencil, ink and colour wash drawing of the Glasgow School of Art showing sections through the studios; prepared by Mackintosh in 1910.
14 A turn-of-the-century photograph taken from the north-west showing the school of art in its original context before the large-scale redevelopment of its surroundings.
15 One of Mackintosh's sketches of Maybole Castle, Ayrshire, 1895. Maybole can be seen as the starting point for the east elevation of the Glasgow School of Art.

16

lights indicate the boardroom while the smallest illumines the models' changing room, Mackintosh has a range of window types which he has some difficulty in uniting so that they may be read as anything like an aesthetic whole. Although the half-protruding tower has been criticized as being non-functional it did indeed house a staircase until the introduction of the east service stair after 1907.[30]

The north elevation sits on the crown of the hill. Early illustrations show that when phase one was completed the block terminated just to the west of the entrance. In striking contrast to the east and west elevations, the north elevation is unyieldingly horizontal except for the jigsaw pieces that make up the centre. Scholars are always playing the game of hunt the source so although it can be accepted that the east and west elevations have in varied measure something of the sheer planes of Scotland's unique heritage of tower-houses, **16**, the north elevation is markedly, perhaps perversely, different with its parade of huge metal windows and the complex geometry of the centrepiece. The obvious parallel is with the Elizabethan prodigy houses and especially Montacute House, Somerset, **17**, which Mackintosh sketched in the summer of 1895. Significantly, Montacute House shows three design features which interested Mackintosh: a three-storeyed front, the top-most treated as a continuous screen; the horizontality interrupted by a central vertical break; and on the return elevation a long dropped window which brings to mind the library windows, **18**, of the Glasgow School of Art.[31] Mackintosh was too complex an artist to imitate. In his mind many concepts must have been swirling. Thus, the compositional asymmetry of the entrance and adjacent window bay, **19**, has been compared by more than one

commentator to Norman Shaw's New Zealand Chambers (1872) and also to sketches by Mackintosh when on holiday on the south coast of England. As fenestration is used by Mackintosh to express internal functional hierarchies, the lower and smaller window lights what was the janitor's office while the larger window with a balcony bespeaks the authority and dignity of the Director whose command post is symbolized by the metal standard emblematic of the city's coat of arms. As with the undulating verticality of the centre so, too, there are tricks in the long frontal screen. The entrance is on the axis; but the number of window bays varies in the opposing halves. There is a further sleight of hand at the boundary between the street and the domain of the art school where the rhythm of stone piers and railings is at variance with the divisions of the wall plane. In an 1897 drawing of the east elevation a stretch of railing is not only enclosed by a stone cope but has vegetative ornamentation. That this was done away with was because Mackintosh looked at two sources, the Ladbroke Grove Free Library (1890) and the Mary Ward Settlement, Tavistock Square, **20**. Both London buildings have upward sweeps of railings but they have a *fin de siècle* look. Mackintosh's more abstract forms belong to the new century although it was a very long time before it was discovered that the pierced metal discs rising through bunched leaves were Japanese heraldic symbols, **21**.

One of the notable external views of the art school is the junction of the north and west façades with the horizontality of the one played against the verticality of the other. In the ten years since the first phase had begun Mackintosh had matured as an architect. An 1897 design for the west elevation is not dissimilar to the east although the

16 Maybole Castle, Ayrshire: a typical Scottish tower-house.
17 Montacute House, Somerset, 1590–1600.
18 Library window, Glasgow School of Art.
19 Compositional asymmetry in the entrance and adjacent window bay, Glasgow School of Art.

20 The Mary Ward Settlement, Tavistock Square, London, Smith and Brewer, 1895–98.
21 Railing detail, Glasgow School of Art; the pierced metal discs rising through bunched leaves are derived from Japanese heraldic symbols.

18

19

17

20

21

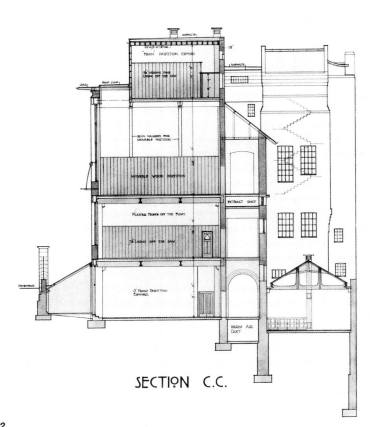

SECTION C.C.

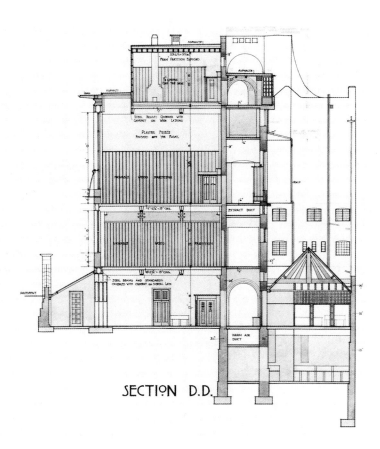

SECTION D.D.

22 Pencil, ink and colour wash drawing of the Glasgow School of Art, prepared by Mackintosh in 1910.

22

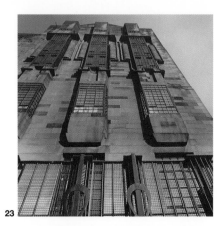

23

24

23 The school of art
library windows soar,
uninterrupted, through
three floors.
24 Detail of the
entrance to Scott Street:
a proto-Art Deco
composition.
25 The great show
front of Fyvie Castle,
Aberdeenshire, as
published in MacGibbon
and Ross' *Domestic and*

*Castellated Architecture
of Scotland*.
26 Pencil, ink and
colour wash drawing
of the school, south
elevation, prepared by
Mackintosh in 1910.
27 Drawing prepared
by Mackintosh in March
1897 showing the east
and west elevations and
an early version of the
library façade.

fenestration is more cohesive and can be seen to be leading on to the final resolution. The ten year hiatus gave Mackintosh assurance enough to defy his own early logic of allying fenestration to internal space so that the library windows soar without interruption through three floors, **23**. What was the source of the change? Possibly, the rear elevation of the Bristol Reference Library as depicted in 1905 in *The Builder*[32] for like any good and not so good architect Mackintosh would have scanned the journals to see what others were about. By studying the drawings prepared between 1897 and 1910 one can grasp the additive nature of Mackintosh's architecture and its organic development. Thus, in the 1907 drawings Mackintosh sketched the figurative carving intended for the library niches probably in expectation of the £1,000 'entered in the masonwork contract for carving'.[33] By that time there had already been a disagreement about the entrance to the lecture theatre. 'On leaving a meeting today, six of the Governors inspected a newly erected sub-basement porch and entrance in Scott Street and were surprised to find that this work was carried out in an extravagant manner and not in accordance with the plans and estimates which were submitted and signed'.[34] Today the plane of the curved forewall against the staggered proto-Art Deco geometry of the door surround projecting from recessed planes is one of the most admired features, **24**.

Although Mackintosh would have liked his statues of the arts, their omission is probably a gain. It is the latticed glass, untrammelled by bodily support, like a coruscating coat of mail against the body of stone, which is the abiding vision of the Glasgow School of Art. No wonder that it was used on the front of Sir Nikolaus Pevsner's

Pioneers of Modern Design (1960) along with the slightly later factory at Alfeld-an-der-Leine by Walter Gropius, the Eiffel Tower and Olbrich's Wedding Tower, Darmstadt.

On the west the library windows project; on the south they do not since, in the competition brief, it was stated that 'all breaks and projections… must be confined within the building lines shown on the plan'.[35] Hence the south elevation, always partly obscured by lower buildings along Sauchiehall Street, is composed of unadorned blocks with harling over the brickwork. The play of matt surfaces punctured by few window openings recalls the unrivalled tower-houses of north-east Scotland which have been described as 'a kind of Indian summer of the Middle Ages'.[36] The obvious comparison is with the great show front of Fyvie Castle, **25**, Aberdeenshire, which Mackintosh accepted as 'one of the finest and most characteristic castles in the Scottish style'.[37] To prove that such an allusion is not too far fetched one need only look in the pages of MacGibbon and Ross' *Domestic and Castellated Architecture of Scotland* at Huntly Castle in the same county where as Mackintosh noted, 'In the upper part of this castle we find a very uncommon feature in the three oriel windows'[38] which reappear in the south-west corner of the south elevation of the school of art. It is the south elevation, in its geometrical rationalism, that comes closest to parallels with the Viennese school, particularly Hoffmann's sanatorium at Purkersdorf, Vienna (1903).

Confronted with the Glasgow School of Art, it is easy to forget that Mackintosh was trained in the classical tradition. Thus it was surely not necessity that dictated that the approach into the building should be by an external staircase leading to a *piano nobile* with its hall and the

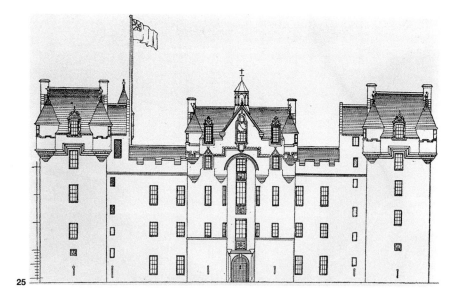

25

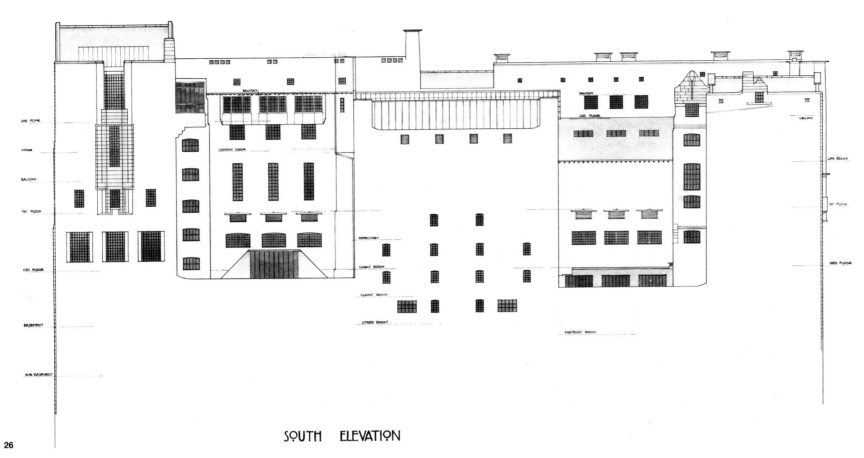

SOUTH ELEVATION

EAST
ELEVATION

WEST
ELEVATION

SECTION
THROUGH
LIBRARY

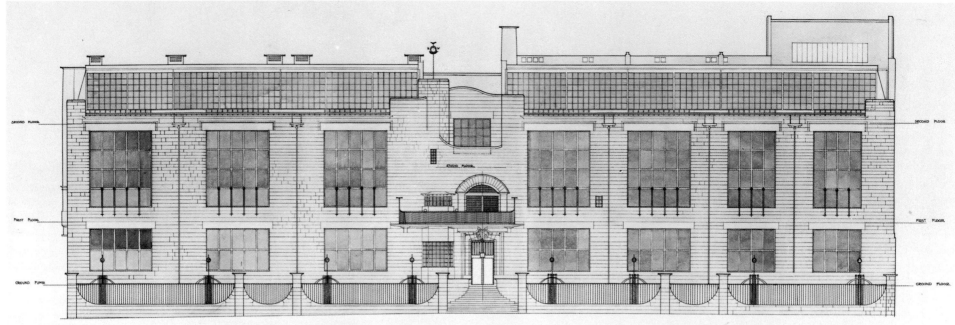

28

28 Pencil, ink and colour wash drawing of the school of art, elevation to Renfrew Street, prepared by Mackintosh in 1910.
29 The entrance hall photographed shortly after the school's completion.
30 The entrance hall and staircase to the first-floor museum.

31 Detail of the timber roof structure which grows out of and spreads above the main staircase.
32 An early view of the corridor outside the life modelling room; before firedoors were installed there existed a continuous vista along the building from east to west.

29

30

31

museum above as the saloon. It is by means of space and light that the visitor is drawn up to the museum from the entrance threshold which originally, as can be seen on the 1910 drawing, was an open porch, with entry controlled from the janitor's box, with a central timber post which, like a tree, carries a sculpture emblematic of knowledge and art, **28**.

Early photographs demonstrate the drama of the hallway, **29**, where the impression is of Piranesi's *carceri* with square piers, oppressive grey concrete vaults and light spilling down the staircase from the museum. Today, the hall does not perhaps gain from the overall whiteness, the evenness of the artificial lighting or the mosaic infilling of the niches with a pantheon of artists and architects including Wren and Mackintosh. It is in the hall that one first experiences that subdivision of space within space by the use of the line of piers to direct the route to the staircase, **30**.

In a lecture on Elizabethan architecture Mackintosh described the staircase at Crewe Hall, Cheshire: 'It is a newel stair built round a central well hole, and is of oak… and occupies but little space, being not more than 24 ft square from wall to wall while the storey itself is 20 feet high'.[39] These are almost the same dimensions as the staircase of the Glasgow School of Art. Although Mackintosh eschews all historical detail he cannot avoid contemporary associations. The newel posts with flat caps are derived doubtless from Mackmurdo's Century Guild stand at the Liverpool International Exhibition in 1886 while the continuation of the corner posts to form a cage has a parallel with Voysey's staircase at Broadleys, Lake Windermere (1898).

Early photographs show the museum to have been a more interesting space than it is today since a uniform brownness was introduced in the 1970s probably without recourse either to historical documents or to those who might have made a knowledgeable contribution. Mackintosh intended the space to be read with wood-lined walls meeting the revealed construction of stone coursing, exposed concrete arches over the corridor entrances and a timber roof structure which grows out of and spreads above the staircase, **31**.

The Director's room is separated from the museum by a high dark anteroom which, with its low benches, seems to have been designed expressly to lower the spirits of those members of the student body summoned for interview. The door opens and there is a burst of light from both the window in its alcove and from the white walls, **33**. The shape of the room with the alcove flowing out of a square is a powerful reminder of the interiors scooped out of the walls in Scottish castles and in particular of some of the upper rooms in Castle Campbell, Clackmannanshire, which Mackintosh mentioned in his lecture.

Before firedoors were installed in the corridors it was possible to appreciate a continuous vista from east to west and the subtle interflow of the long, narrow spaces with the museum. The corridors, **34**, are the service routes leading to the studios along the north side, to the (original) boardroom and to the library in the south-east and south-west corners respectively where subsidiary service stairs were added at the insistence of the fire authorities in phase two. Originally there was the central staircase only. When Mackintosh was sketching Montacute House did he have an opportunity to study the plan which approximates to the early layout of the Glasgow School of Art?

32

33

34

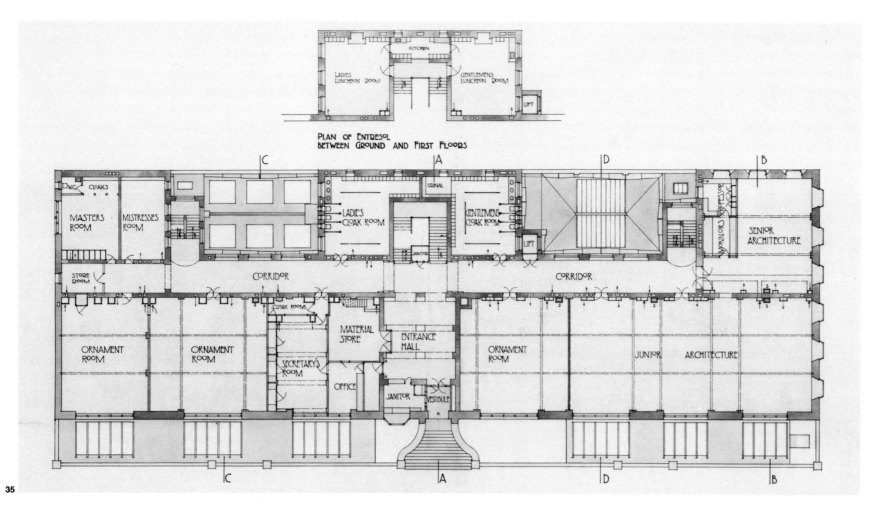

PLAN OF ENTRESOL
BETWEEN GROUND AND FIRST FLOORS

35

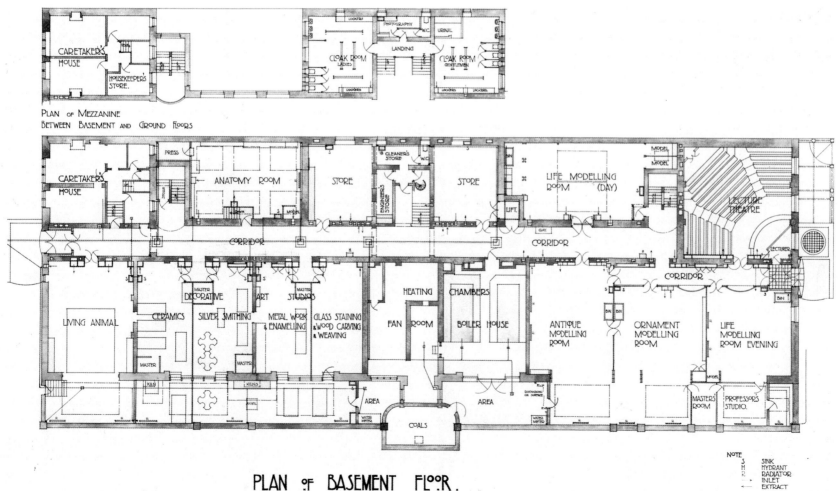

PLAN OF MEZZANINE
BETWEEN BASEMENT AND GROUND FLOORS

PLAN OF BASEMENT FLOOR.

36

35–38 Pencil, ink and colour wash renderings of the basement, ground, first and second floor plans of the Glasgow School of Art, prepared by Mackintosh in 1910.

37

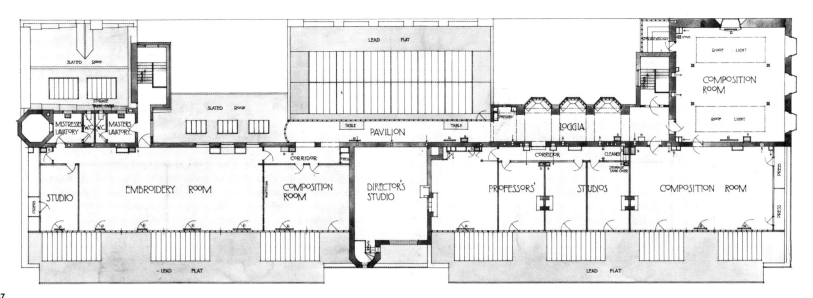

PLAN OF MEZZANINE
BETWEEN FIRST AND SECOND FLOORS

PLAN OF LIBRARY BALCONY

38

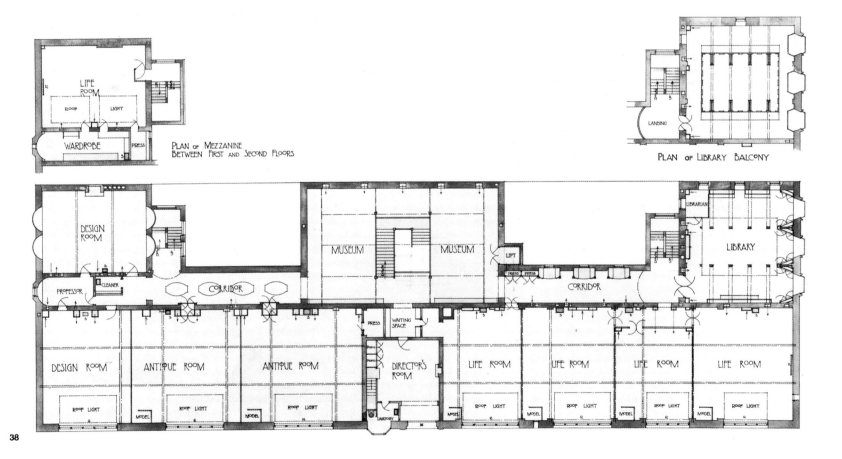

39

And is it a coincidence that with dark timber and plaster above so much of the interior looks Elizabethan? That is so even in the studios with their grid of mullions and transoms spanning the length of the north wall with more light gained from above by glazing between the rafters. In the former life modelling studio in the basement the rafters are so thickly clustered as almost to exclude light, **39**. It is here that the ends of the T-girders are split and forged into patterns, the making of which is said to have caused the blacksmiths to strike. With these, as with the brackets on the windows of the north studios, one sees Mackintosh as the follower of the Arts and Crafts movement.

The second phase

In the second building phase the (original) boardroom became the design room and is now the Mackintosh room, **40**. It is used for meetings and the permanent display of furniture and other works by Mackintosh, as well as photographs of The Four and of Mackintosh's principal clients, Newbery and his wife, William Davidson, who commissioned Windyhill (1899), Walter Blackie of The Hill House (1902) and Miss Cranston, the restauranteur, some of whose tea-room furniture is among the exhibits. Although Mackintosh's furniture was always designed for specific settings this collection is not only set off well but gives some understanding of his development as a furniture designer. The earliest piece, dating from c.1896, is a linen cupboard, stained green, with brass hinges commissioned by W. Davidson. Interestingly, an early article in The Studio reported that, 'Some stains for wood, manufactured by Mr H.H. Stephens, whose ebony stain,

intended for articles of furniture and the like, has become the most favourite fluid for ordinary drawings for reproduction, are distinctly good. The green is vivid, yet exactly the right colour to look well on oak or pine'.[40] The large oak bookcase from the drawing-room at Windyhill is of interest since beside it there hangs Mackintosh's scale drawing with the few measurements which were perhaps all that was given to the cabinetmaker. The most magnificent item is a gesso panel by Margaret Macdonald entitled 'The Heart of the Rose'. Its depiction of women cradling a child is as powerful as a Madonna and Child by an Italian master.

The (original) boardroom, though simplicity itself, has much subtlety beginning with the two axes. The first is east–west and is determined by the pair of bowed windows in each external wall. Above, however, are the transverse divisions of the steel beams coated with cement on wire lath. What the casual visitor will not notice is that the door jambs are free-standing and tapering with inserts of stained glass in the doors. Indeed, there is scarcely a door in the building that does not have stained glass, **42**, whether it be rosebuds for the studios, butterflies, swifts, seed pods or embryonic female forms as on the secretary's door. It is such craft details that must have contributed to the over-run on the budget.

With phase two changes of use were made to some parts of the building. The boardroom became a design space, the museum was no longer a studio (in 1903 it had been partitioned for the antique class) and the eastern staircase, at the end of the first-floor corridor and expressed externally by the half enclosed turret, became redundant when the new east and west staircases were inserted. Sensibly and

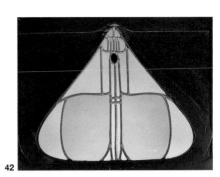

42

40

41

39 An early photograph of the life modelling room, located in the basement, c.1910.
40 The Mackintosh room, originally the boardroom; frosted glass in the bow windows on the west wall conceal the east staircase, added when the building was extended in 1909.
41 The staircase wraps around the existing window bays.
42 A stained glass door panel.

43

ingeniously the western external windows of the (original) boardroom were retained leaving the staircase steps to float around them.

Further insubstantiality was achieved by breaking through the core wall of each staircase perhaps in imitation of the staircase niches at Montacute House or more obviously the great stair at Hardwick Hall, Derbyshire. Each landing or half stage has a pattern of tiles with more at the summit where metal screens criss-cross veiling the transition from the stone walls to the timber roofs, **43**. While Mackintosh's use of screens may owe something to Japanese influences there were Scottish precedents in the yetts or iron grilles with their unique interweaving in alternate quarters of uprights and cross-pieces.

The firestairs are cross-linked at the second floor. Because the Director's studio rises through the centre of the building there could be no direct east–west connection on the second floor. Today there is a corridor in the eastern section, sectioned off from a series of interconnecting studios, from which a dog-leg leads into the pavilion as it is labelled in the 1910 drawings. Very quickly this narrow glazed space, **44**, must have generated the nickname by which it has been known to generations of students – the hen-run – a lightweight construction of wood and glass nestling between the pitch of the museum roof and the south wall of the Director's studio. With the hen-run Mackintosh has devised one of his most memorable spaces. Entering from the stone staircase and the dark passage way one is brought into a transparent capsule floating above the Glasgow townscape and commanding a limitless vista to the southern hills beyond the River Clyde while the near view is of the grid-like tenement blocks interrupted by steeples and towers, including that of Thomson's

St Vincent Street Church. So, what could have been a utilitarian passage has become a pleasure pavilion, a place in which to loiter, for delicate slow movements within the gossamer structure, its fragility emphasized by the slight incline of the glass roof and the curved eastern bow.

Once the hen-run led directly into the loggia, **45**, but today a firedoor reduces the impact of moving from insubstantiality to more solid space. This transition would have been further heightened when the loggia's brickwork was exposed, **46**, and not coated with white emulsion paint, with soft tonal gradations and lines of pointing repeating in diminuendo the patterning of the hen-run. The loggia is made up on plan of three squares covered by groin vaults. The south wall, however, is opened in bays with folding desks to enable students to work. Thus they may gaze from the hen-run at the inheritance of the city that is theirs or in the loggia may capture its forms and silhouettes beneath the sombre skies of the west of Scotland.

To the north of the loggia are the professors' studios. In the convivial life of the art school they have always been more than studios, for Mackintosh created them as generous living spaces made intimate by the boarded walls, open fireplaces and the screen of chequered glass which, set back from the wallhead, further enhances the sense that here is a private domain, **47**.

In the south-east corner is the former flower painting studio with a conservatory cantilevered in space above a series of corbels. At first Newbery had arranged for students to visit the Botanic Gardens, then the suggestion was made that cuttings could be brought to the school and soon a conservatory was established to be retained in phase two.

43 Detail of decorative ironwork balustrade on the east staircase.
44 The 'hen-run', a lightweight construction of wood and glass that runs along the south façade.
45 A contemporary view of the loggia.
46 An early photograph of the loggia, showing the building in its original state before the brickwork was whitewashed, c.1910.
47 The generous living space of a professor's studio in the school of art, c.1910.

44

45

46

47

48

In the studio Mackintosh gave the plants swathes of light from the south, low rays from the west and gentle top-lighting from the north so that the plants could be seen in all its parts. Yet what a contrast between pots and vases and the scale of the studio where once there was exposed creamy stone in the bottom courses with plain brickwork above. Surely a cleverer background than the white paint now daubed over every surface save for the double posts with pegged cross timbers, one of the more obvious borrowings from Japan, which are part of the structural system of the library below.

The top-most stage of the library was a bookstore, **48**, but is now a display area for an accumulation of treasures. Unfortunately, there is nothing by Herbert McNair. Not only was there a fire in his studio before 1897 but after the death of Frances much was destroyed so that any assessment of his merit as an artist is limited to the few dozen items in public or, more rarely, in private collections. Thus it is difficult to assess his impact on the development of The Four although it seems that in certain important respects, especially perhaps in furniture design, it was McNair and not Mackintosh who led the way. Margaret Macdonald is represented by the two panels which once hung on either side of the bed in the master bedroom at Hill House. In these, a mixture of appliqué and other techniques, etiolated women pray for a benison on lovemaking.

The greater part of the collection represents Mackintosh in many of his phases. The earliest two-dimensional work is the north elevation of the 'Grand Hall for International Exhibition 1901' with the last being the watercolour of 'Le Fort, Maillert' (1927) which shows his persistent fondness for cobalt blue often set against viridian. There are also unrealized architectural designs including the project for 'A Country Cottage for an Artist' (1901) now built in Inverness-shire. A substantial number of items are from Miss Cranston's tea-rooms ranging from the chunky oak domino table and chairs from Argyle Street, **49**, to the more sophisticated pieces from the room-de-luxe in the Willow tea-room. These have been restored using dark purple cloth and aluminium paint. How can such insensitive treatment accord with the notion of silvered furnishings?

The library

Now that the bookstore is the furniture gallery and on the visitors' route of the building, they can begin to comprehend the structure of the library. From two cast-iron cross-beams metal hangers are dropped through the floor to reappear in the library below encased in oak and thereby seeming to be supports. That is one illusion in the library which, as the extant drawings show, became ever more complex as the years passed. On paper the structural divisions establish a nave and aisles plan which is entered on a diagonal, thus adding to the visual complexity. The timber posts are seemingly multiplied becoming a grove of trees with the multi-coloured branch-like balusters thrown into relief against the gallery of boarded panels with the ends of some dropped, carved and pierced, **50**. Whereas most practitioners would have tied the gallery to the uprights Mackintosh's separation not only maintains the structural integrity of the main posts but surely gives significance to the balusters. The gallery, which Mackintosh insisted must run on all four sides, rests on pairs of

48 The upper-most stage of the library was originally a book-store but now serves as an exhibition space.
49 A robust oak domino table and set of chairs displayed in the school of art's museum; these were designed by Mackintosh for Miss Cranston's Argyle Street tea-rooms.
50 The forest-like structure of the library.

49

50

brackets projected to embrace the balusters and is then clamped to the oak upright. It is a device which Mackintosh may have observed in the gallery of Queen Margaret College (now the John Mcintyre Building). Designed by J.J. Burnet (1887, extended 1895) it was only a few hundred yards from Mackintosh's home overlooking the University of Glasgow.

Most of the natural lighting comes from the fugue of windows which, bursting through their physical boundaries of height and depth, defy space almost like the Five Sisters window at York Minster. At Scotland Street School the staircases are withheld from the outer screen of glass producing a void, **51**, **52**; at the art school the hexagonal void links the outer and the inner transparencies. Before the monstrous bulk of the school of architecture was built across the street the low light of an afternoon and early evening would percolate the interstices of the carved pendants before falling across the inner screen of posts and the furniture. The sturdy oak chairs, designed by Mackintosh, have been brought in from the Ingram Street tea-room. The original chairs, of which only six remain, are low enough to fit beneath the tables so that their spindly forms and the table legs, pierced and carved to match the pendant boards, become like thickets beneath the spreading canopy above.

The umbered tones of the library and its three-dimensional structural forms can be appreciated by all. Yet what does it all mean? Why are the pendant boards of the gallery pierced? What is the significance, if any, of the massed central lamps, **53**, with their glass inserts? Why are the colours so at variance with the primary colours of the balusters? These disparities should worry anyone acquainted

not only with the unity of Mackintosh's interiors but with his interest in symbolism. Perhaps in designing the library Mackintosh had in mind the Ladbroke Free Library, London. Aside from the railings and the gridded windows what could have held Mackintosh's attention would have been the external, three-dimensional carving of the Tree of Knowledge although he might have found the representation of the subject too anthropomorphic. Yet in 1896 McNair had designed a bookplate with a similar union of women and 'the tree of knowledge which enfolds with its branches the spirits of art and poetry'[41]; and in the Buchanan Street tea-room Mackintosh's frieze (now destroyed) had women so enmeshed by briar roses as to be imprisoned. Later the room-de-luxe in the Willow tea-room was conceived around the lines by D.G. Rossetti:

Oh ye, all ye that walk in Willowwood,
That walk with hollow faces burning bright,

lines which were fulfilled in Margaret Macdonald's gesso panel. On the ground floor the plaster frieze, devoid of human figures, has a ghostly depth as one stick-like form fades behind another. Trees appear too in Mackintosh's watercolours, most mysteriously in the 'The Tree of Personal Effort' and 'The Tree of Influence' (1895). As a critic wrote of such work at the time: 'To delight in improbables and fancies, in symbolism and imagination, which find expression in subjects that are certainly not easily interpreted by the careless spectator may be only the inevitable reaction from a period of realism and naturalistic impressions'.[42]

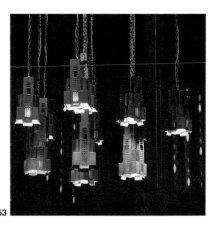

53

51 SCHOOL BOARD OF GLASGOW SCOTLAND STREET PVBLIC SCHOOL.

52

51 A perspective rendering of Scotland Street School prepared by W.S. Moyes in 1904.
52 Scotland Street School, detail of the staircase window; the staircases are withheld from the outer screen of glass, producing a void similar, in effect, to the library windows of the school of art.
53 A group of Mackintosh-designed lamps in the library.

How then should the library of the Glasgow School of Art be interpreted? As a grove of trees perhaps with the light penetrating the leaf forms of the pendants and the white, green, red and blue colours of the four seasons in the balusters above spreading beyond the oak trunks. The central floor space is open; lights shine down. Suspended from long chains over the central table, for which 'the architect was asked to submit a design for a magazine rack' in 1909,[43] a cluster of black and silver lamps, like miniature skyscrapers have glass inserts of purple and heliotrope.

Perhaps Mackintosh had Lethaby in mind when he wrote of the tabernacle where 'the veil with its tissue of hyacinth, purple, scarlet and fine linen recalled the elements, and divided the outer temple from the sanctuary, as the earth is divided from the heavens'.[44] Is one looking at sanctuary lamps casting their holy light into a sacred grove dedicated to knowledge? If that supposition is correct then the library of the Glasgow School of Art is not only an aesthetic experience but the translation of philosophical thought into three dimensions. What a pity then that one cannot explain the rationale behind the carvings on the Ionic pilasters (and why be so overtly classical?) inset into the panelled walls of the boardroom. Perhaps they are musical notation as has sometimes been thought.

When the second phase of the school of art was handed over in 1909 Mackintosh was present and was praised by Sir John Stirling Maxwell. 'He had shown that it was possible to have a good building without plastering it over with the traditional, expensive and often, ugly ornament.'[45] There was, however, no comment in the professional journals, an omission which is all the more surprising given the coverage of some of Mackintosh's earlier commissions. Yet no photograph of the finished school of art appeared until 1924 when Charles Marriott gave his opinion that the Glasgow School of Art was 'important because of the great influence of Mr Mackintosh's work on the continent – in Germany, Holland and Sweden. It is hardly too much to say that the whole modernist movement in European architecture derives from him'.[46] Perhaps that makes the absence of a published plan until 1950 all the more surprising.[47]

Today the Glasgow School of Art is one of the best known buildings of the twentieth century. Yet is it of the twentieth century? Surely the relationship of ornament to design is a telling commentary on the preaching of Pugin and Ruskin, every hand-made detail a product of the Arts and Crafts movement? And is there such technological and structural innovation? For these should one not look at the reinforced concrete Lion Chambers (1904) by Mackintosh's friend James Salmon? Yet given the poetry of the art school, the glittering façade of the library windows, the mystery of its internal life, the command of spatial complexities, the union of simplicity and sophistication, one has a poetic masterpiece which appeals to the chords of the human spirit. On a practical level too, the building appeals.

It is now nigh on one hundred years since the building was begun. The brief was well put together and the erstwhile student gave a building which without any major changes is today still a working art school, even if the students and staff do have to rub shoulders with tourists.

54 An early view of the library taken before the Mackintosh-designed magazine rack and reading desk was installed, c.1909.

54

Photographs

Previous spread,
Glasgow School of Art
seen from the north-
west: Mackintosh plays
the horizontality of the
north elevation against
the verticality of the west
which is dominated
by the upward sweep
of the library windows.
The large studio
windows benefit from
almost constant
north light.
Left, Mackintosh's
treatment of the façades
allows the honest
expression of the
volumes within,
hence the boardroom
is signalled on the east
elevation by a pair of tall
bow-fronted lights while
the plain windows below
indicate the caretaker's
house.
Right, detail of the
window to the
secretary's room
(originally a professor's
room) adjacent to the
boardroom, now known
as the Mackintosh room.

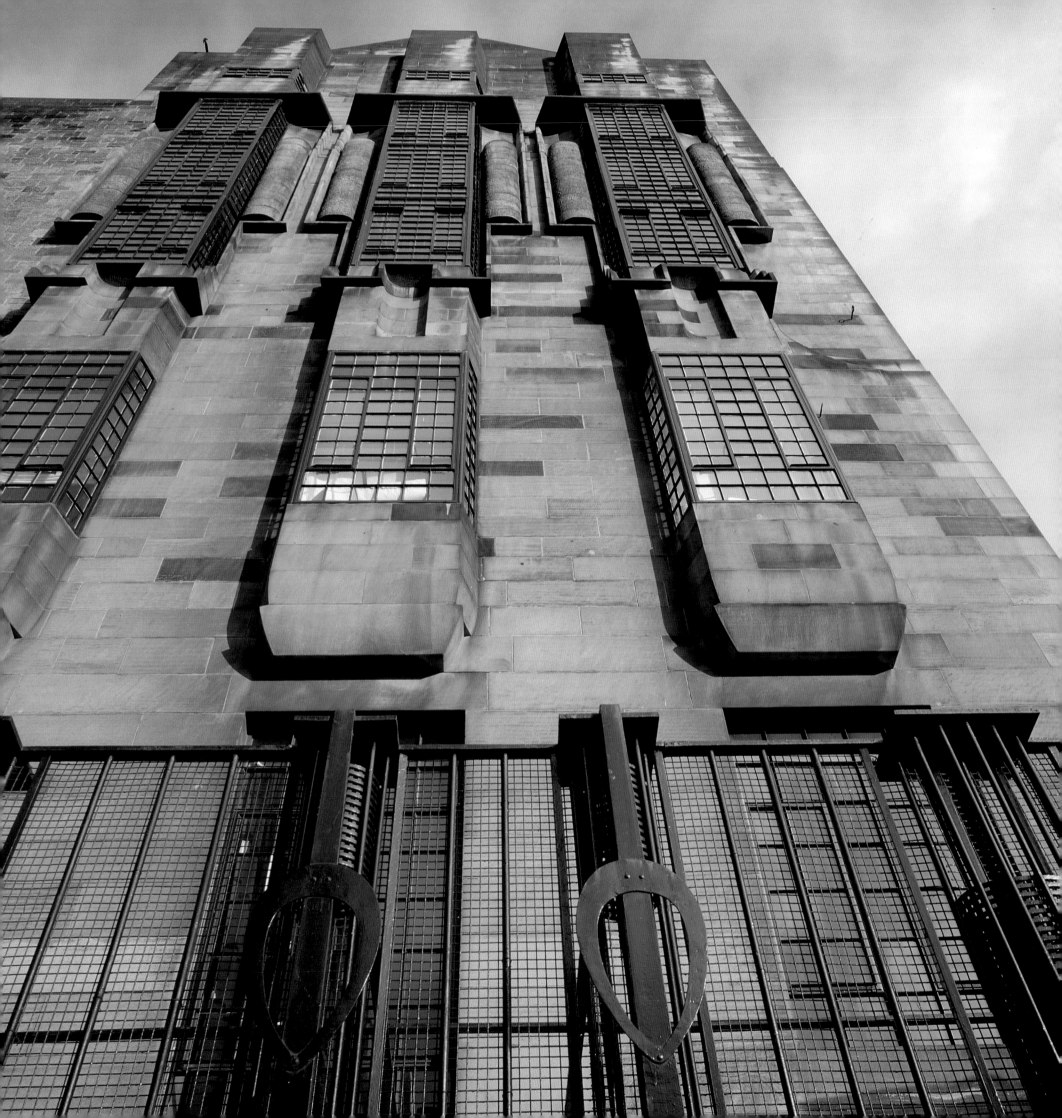

Previous spread, details of the proto-Art Deco sub-basement porch on the west front and the soaring trilogy of windows which light the library above. Left, from the entrance hall, a staircase leads to the school museum, now used as an exhibition space. Right, details of the light fittings in the museum, the staircase balustrade and the timber trussed roof structure which rises out of and spreads above the staircase.

Left, the Director's suite is entered via an intimately-scaled anteroom which mediates between the sombre scale of the museum and the brilliant lightness of the Director's room. Right, view along the first-floor corridor which leads from the museum to the library. Before firedoors were installed in the passageways, it was possible to appreciate a continuous vista from east to west and the subtle interflow of these long narrow spaces with the great volume of the museum.

Opposite, the panelled boardroom on the ground floor created by Mackintosh before the second phase of works of 1907–9. Mackintosh inserted this room within a ground-floor studio next to the general office; it is the only example of his work in the neo-classical style to be completed after 1900. Each of the eight fluted pilasters incorporates a different stylized Ionic motif thought by some to derive from musical notation.

Right, views of the former life modelling studio in the basement. The rafters are thickly clustered so as almost to exclude light. The ends of the T-girders are split and forged into patterns, the manufacture of which is said to have caused the blacksmiths to strike.

The school of art library is Mackintosh's *tour-de-force*. In the centre hangs a cluster of decorative lamps with coloured glass inserts which form a soft counterpoint to the primary colours of the balusters. The oak chairs were made for the Ingram Street tea-room and brought here when that establishment closed. The original library chairs, of which only six now exist, are low enough to fit beneath the tables, their spindly forms and the legs of the tables combining to form thickets beneath the spreading tree-like canopy of the gallery structure.

Left, the library viewed
from the gallery;
the complexity and
intricacy of the detailing
belies the intimate scale
of the room.
Right, the top-most
stage of the library was
originally used for book
storage but is now
a display area for the
school's collection
of Mackintosh furniture
and drawings. The oak
domino table and chairs
were designed for
Miss Cranston's
Argyle Street tea-room.

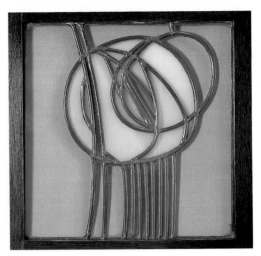

Far left, the Director's
room was one of
Mackintosh's first 'white'
rooms; visitors are
greeted by a flood
of daylight from the
window in its deeply
set alcove.
Right, the Mackintosh
room was originally
designed as a board-
room but became a
drawing studio following
the expansion of the
building in 1907–9.
It contains an extensive
collection of furniture
and ornament designed
by Mackintosh and
Margaret Macdonald.
The lamp and stained-
glass panel, inset left,
are typical of the
ornament and richness
to be found here
and elsewhere in
the building.

Left, located high on the south elevation, the 'hen-run' as it is known popularly, is a lightweight construction of wood and glass. It offers stunning views across the city and forms a route between the dark passageway at the eastern end of the second floor and the loggia.
Right, the loggia forms a substantial counterpoint to the delicacy and lightness of the hen-run. The brick-vaulted structure opens up on the south side to form glazed bays with folding desks to enable students to sit and work.

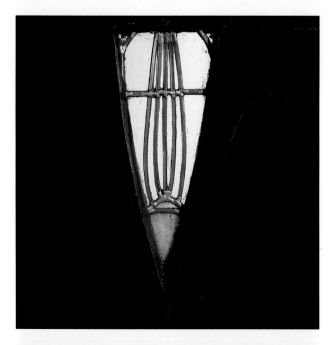

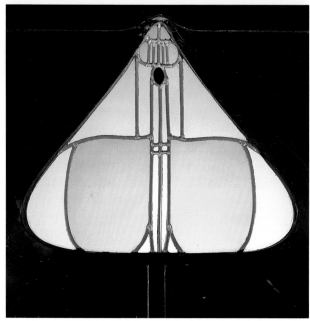

BOARD ROOM

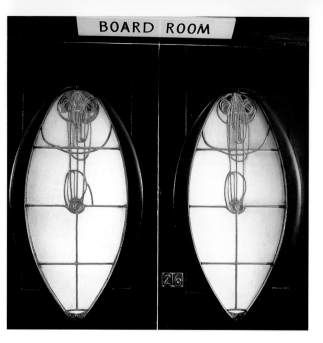

Left, Mackintosh designed leaded glass panels for almost every door in the school of art. The motifs vary from rosebuds, for the studios, butterflies, swifts, seed pods and embryonic female forms. Right, the western escape staircase, incorporated when the school was extended in 1907–9, features elaborate cage-like wrought iron balustrading. Mackintosh's decoration in these utilitarian areas is naturally more modest than in the set-piece spaces, relying mostly on coloured ceramic tiles inset in the plasterwork.

Mackintosh's ironwork, as exemplified here by the window cleaning guards and railings, is startlingly novel and complex. The pierced metal discs rising through clusters of leaves which form a recurring motif on the front railings, derive from Japanese heraldic devices.

Drawings

Site plan and location plan

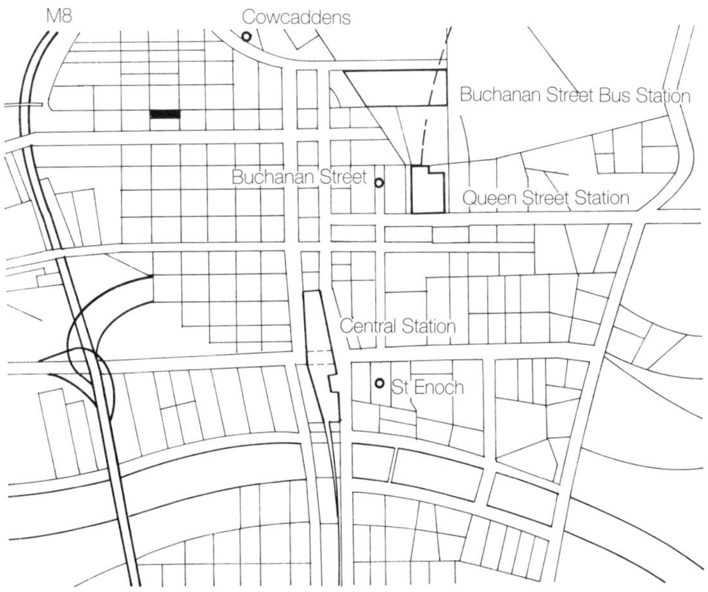

M8
Cowcaddens
Buchanan Street Bus Station
Buchanan Street
Queen Street Station
Central Station
St Enoch

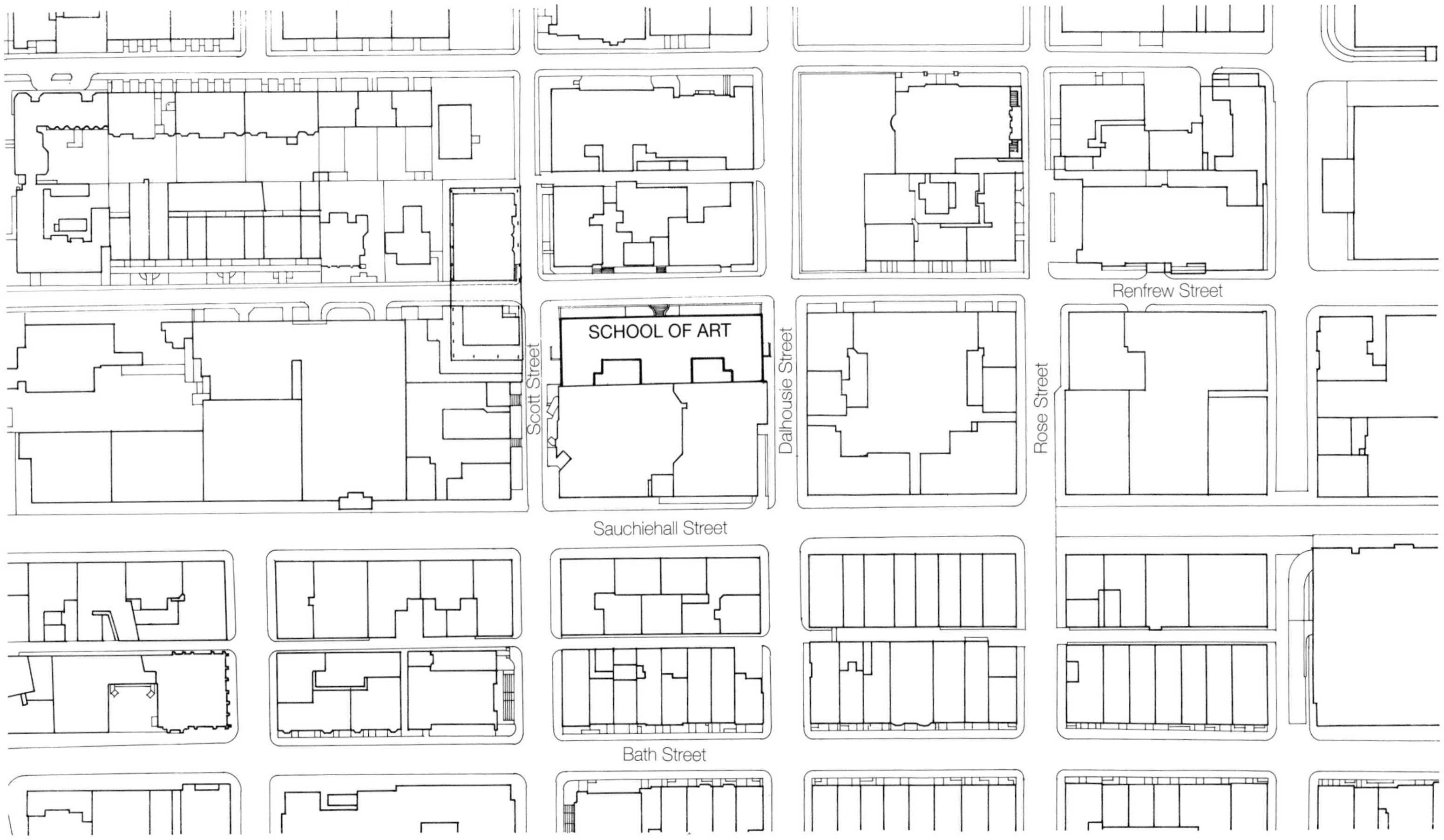

Renfrew Street
SCHOOL OF ART
Scott Street
Dalhousie Street
Rose Street
Sauchiehall Street
Bath Street

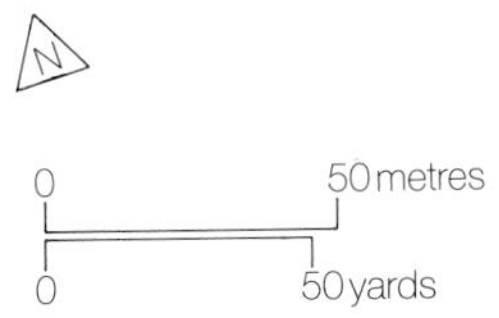

N
0
50 metres
0
50 yards

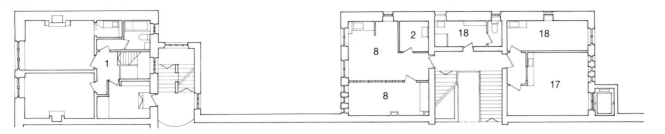

Basement mezzanine

Floor plans
Note: key to floor plans
appears on the following
drawing spread

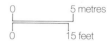

0   5 metres

0   15 feet

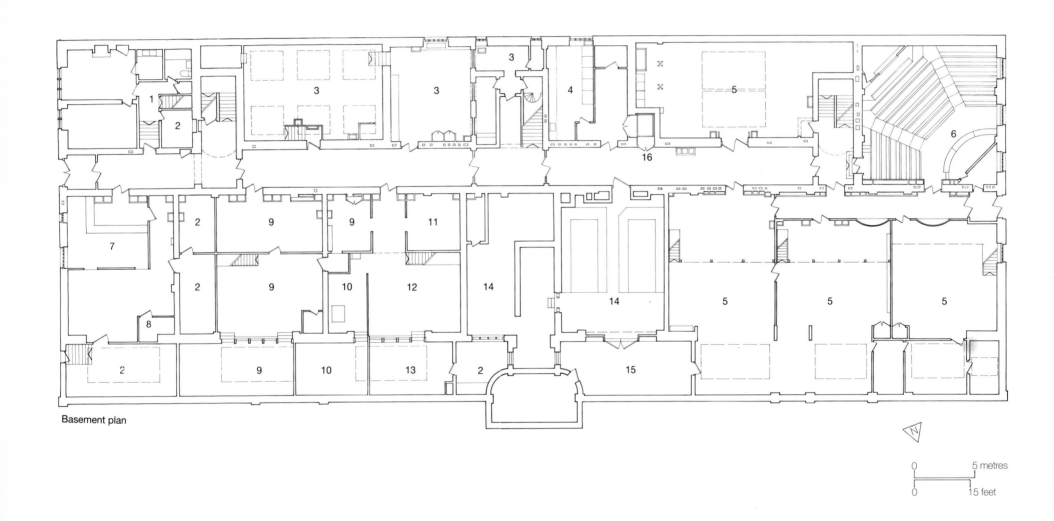

Basement plan

N

0   5 metres

0   15 feet

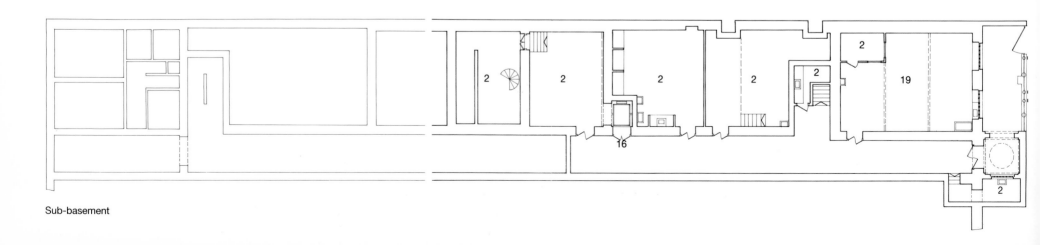

Sub-basement

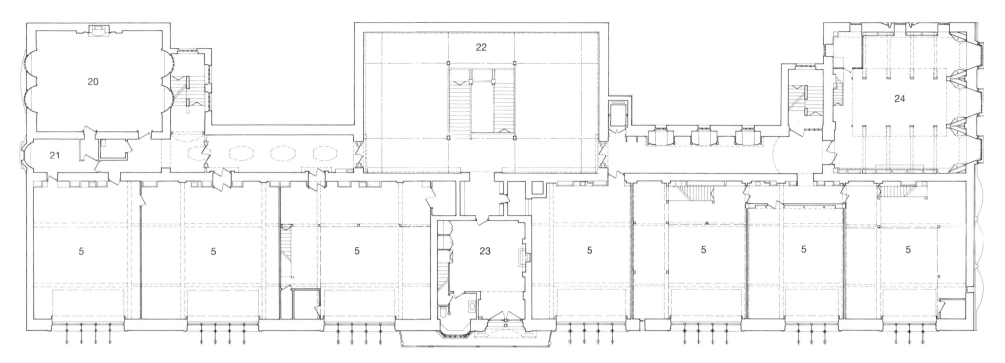

First floor plan

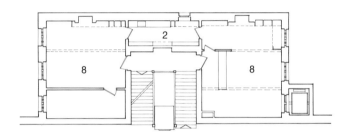

Ground floor mezzanine

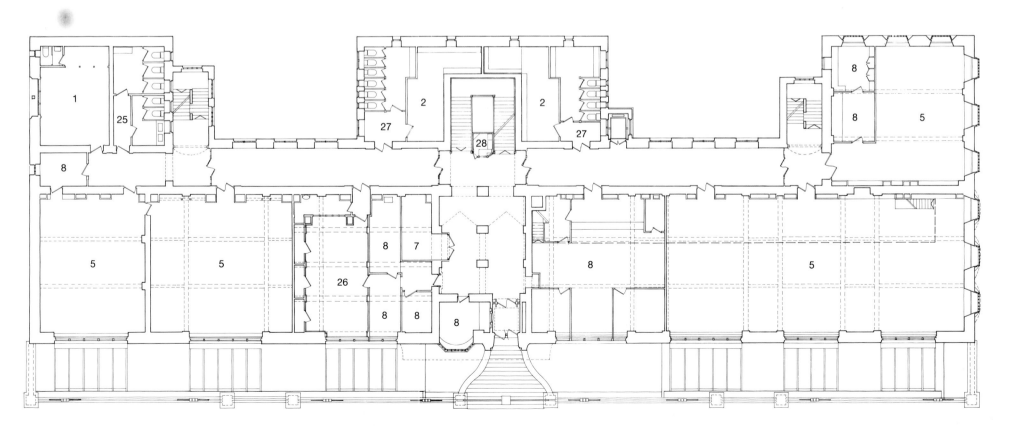

Ground floor plan

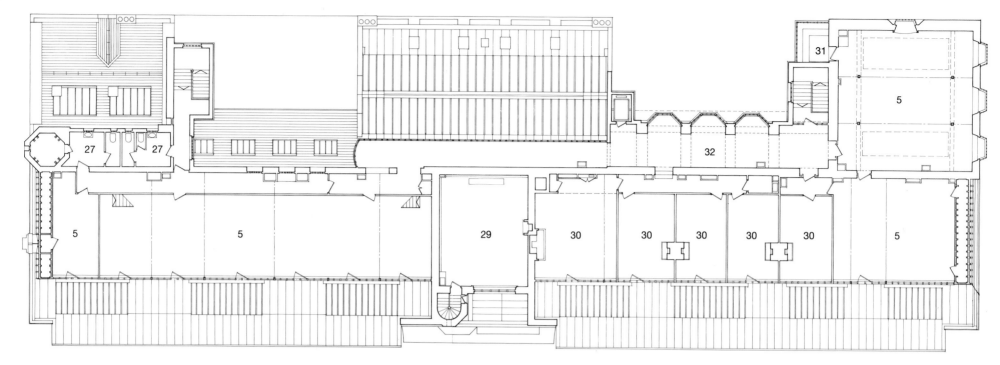

Second floor plan

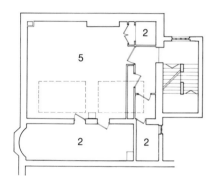

First floor mezzanine: rooflit studio

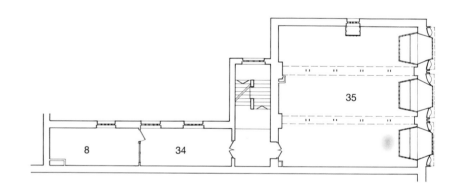

First floor mezzanine above library balcony

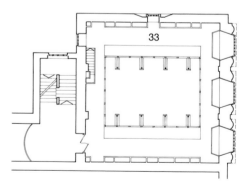

Library balcony

**Key to plans and
sections**

1 visitor's flat
2 store
3 technicians' room
4 photography
5 studio
6 lecture theatre
7 shop
8 office
9 screen printing
10 ceramics
11 clay
12 plaster room
13 modelling
14 plant and boiler
15 well
16 lift
17 janitors' mess
18 models' changing
    room
19 workshop
20 Mackintosh room
21 Director's secretary
22 exhibition space
    (Mackintosh
    Museum)
23 Director's room
24 library
25 staff toilets
26 boardroom
27 toilets
28 janitor/reception
29 Director's studio
30 professors' studios
31 conservatory
32 loggia
33 library balcony
34 computer room
35 Mackintosh curator's
    office and furniture
    store/museum

0   5 metres

0   15 feet

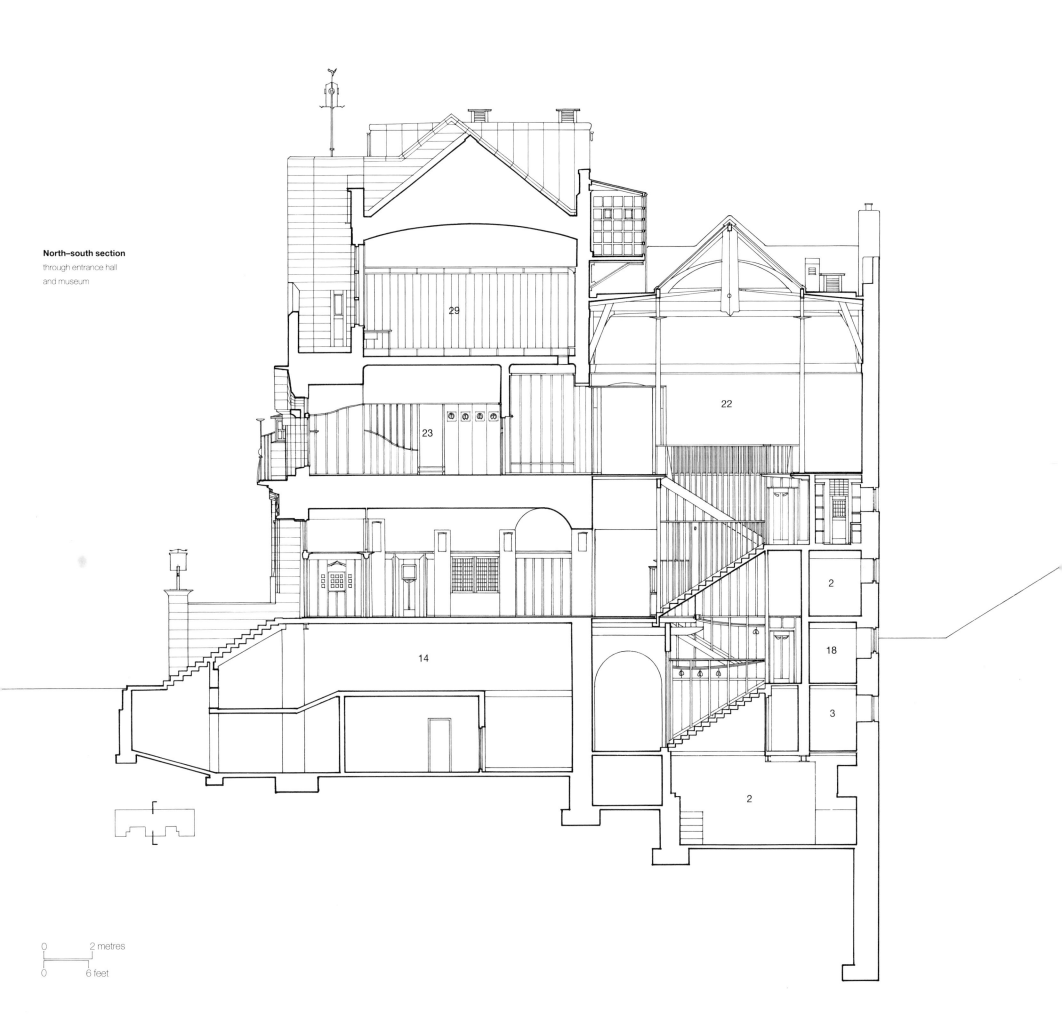

North–south section

through entrance hall
and museum

29

23

22

2

18

3

14

2

0   2 metres

0   6 feet

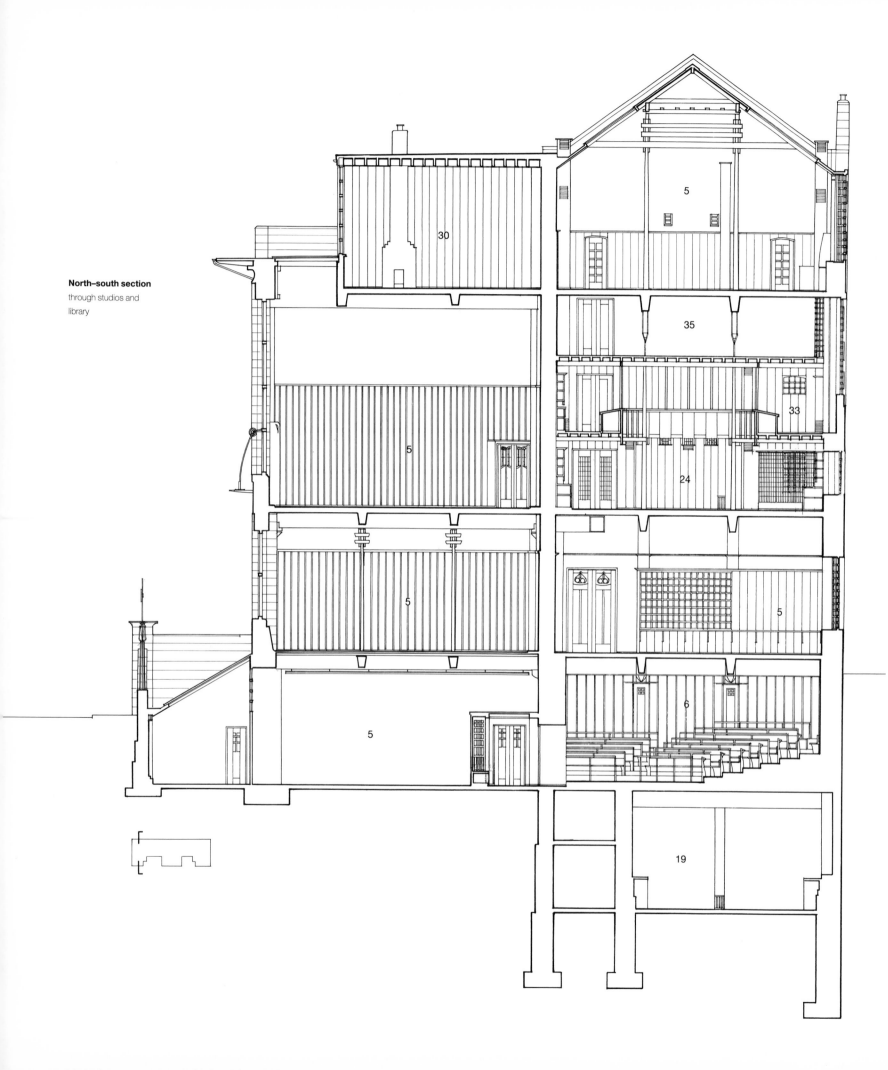

North–south section
through studios and
library

**Details of doorway to
first-floor studio**

1 rose motif stained
glass panels

2 niche

3 60 x 40mm stained
pine batts on plaster
and lath for fixing
collection of plaster
casts

4 200mm stained pine
edge

5 260 x 25mm pine
panelling battens
at 800mm
approximately
vertically on
brickwork wall;
cornice and skirting;
all stained dark

6 bomber hinges to
outer door; floor
springs to both

7 590mm thick brick
wall arch forming
opening

8 875 x 25mm
t & g flooring

9 65 x 150mm stained
pine main posts

10 225 x 25mm stained
pine panels on batts
with 15 x 35mm
semi-circular trims

11 recessed skirting

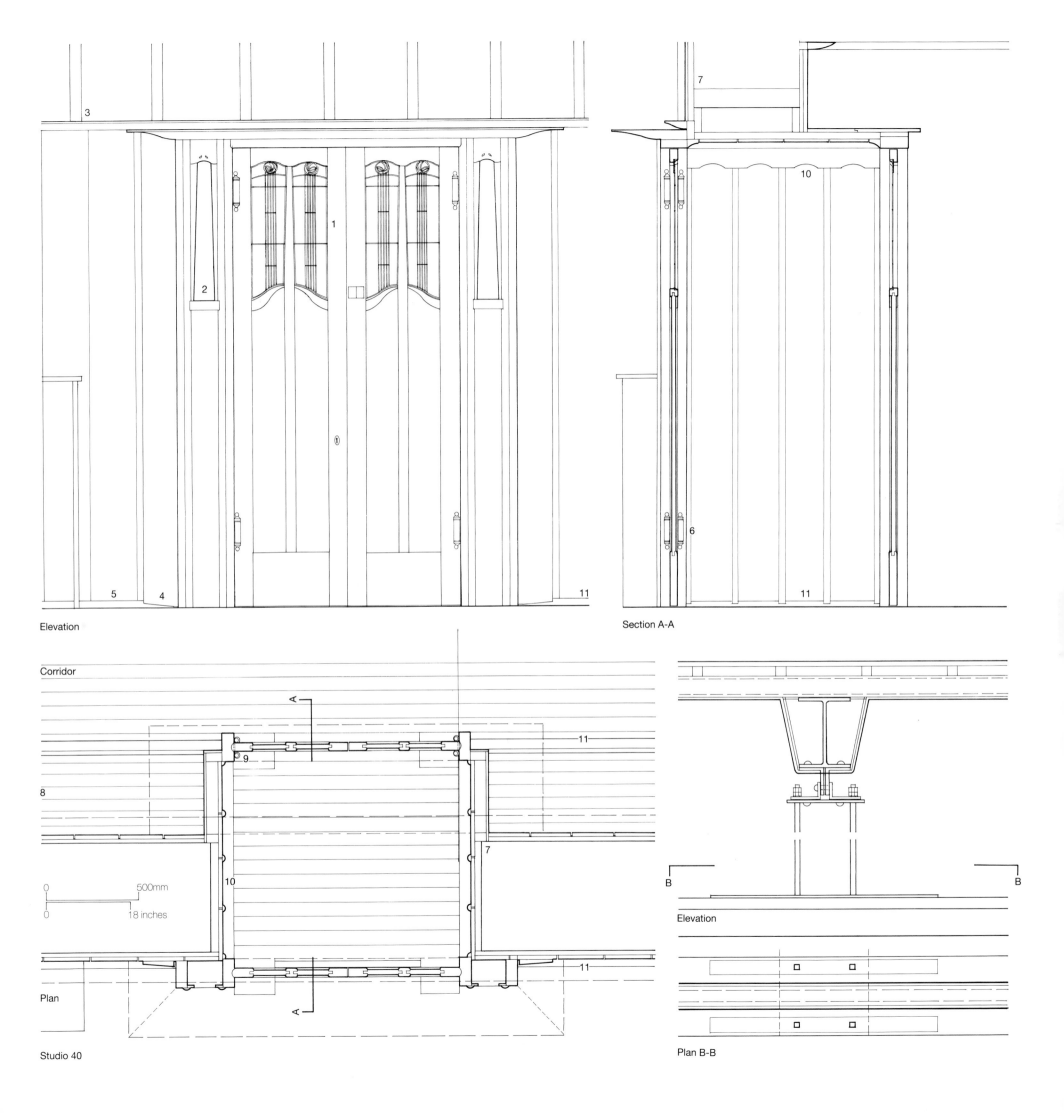

Elevation

Section A-A

Corridor

A

11

9

8

7

10

0   500mm
0   18 inches

Plan

A

11

Studio 40

B   B

Elevation

B   B

Plan B-B

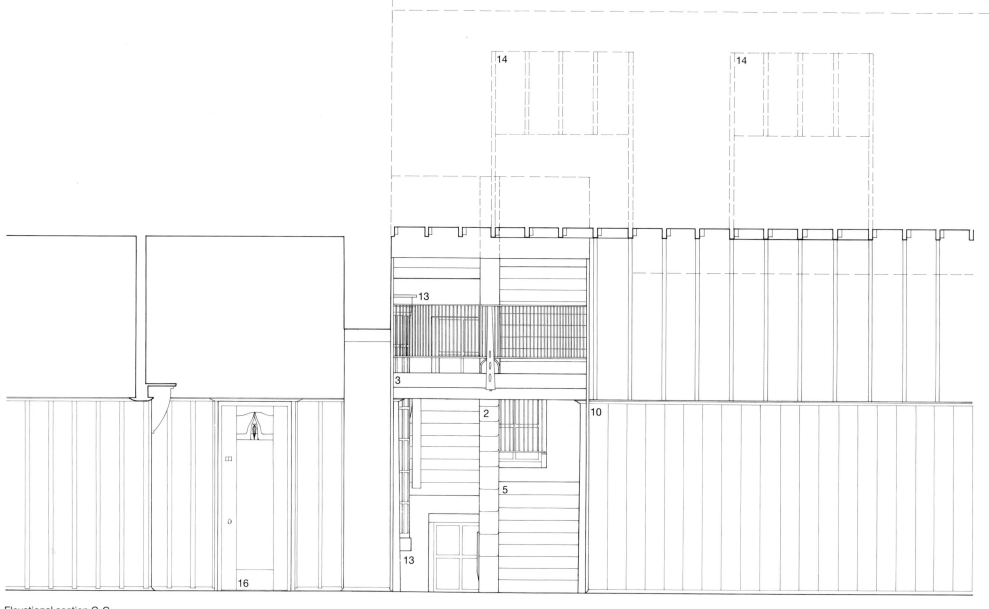

Elevational section C-C

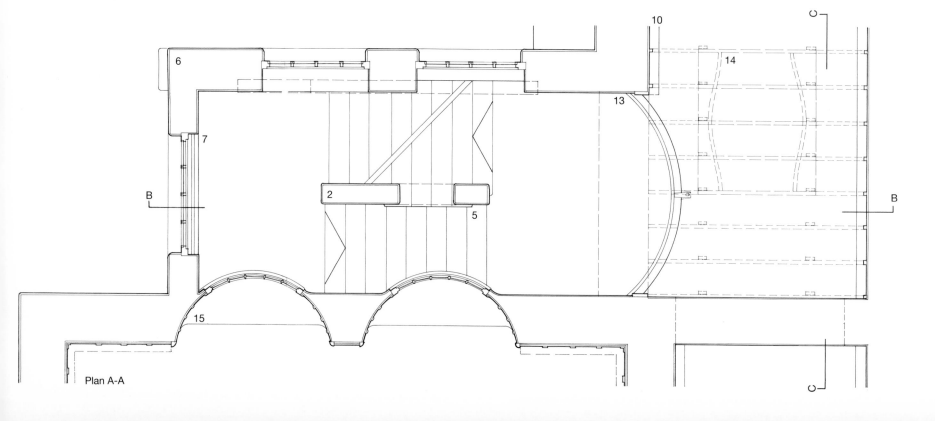

Plan A-A

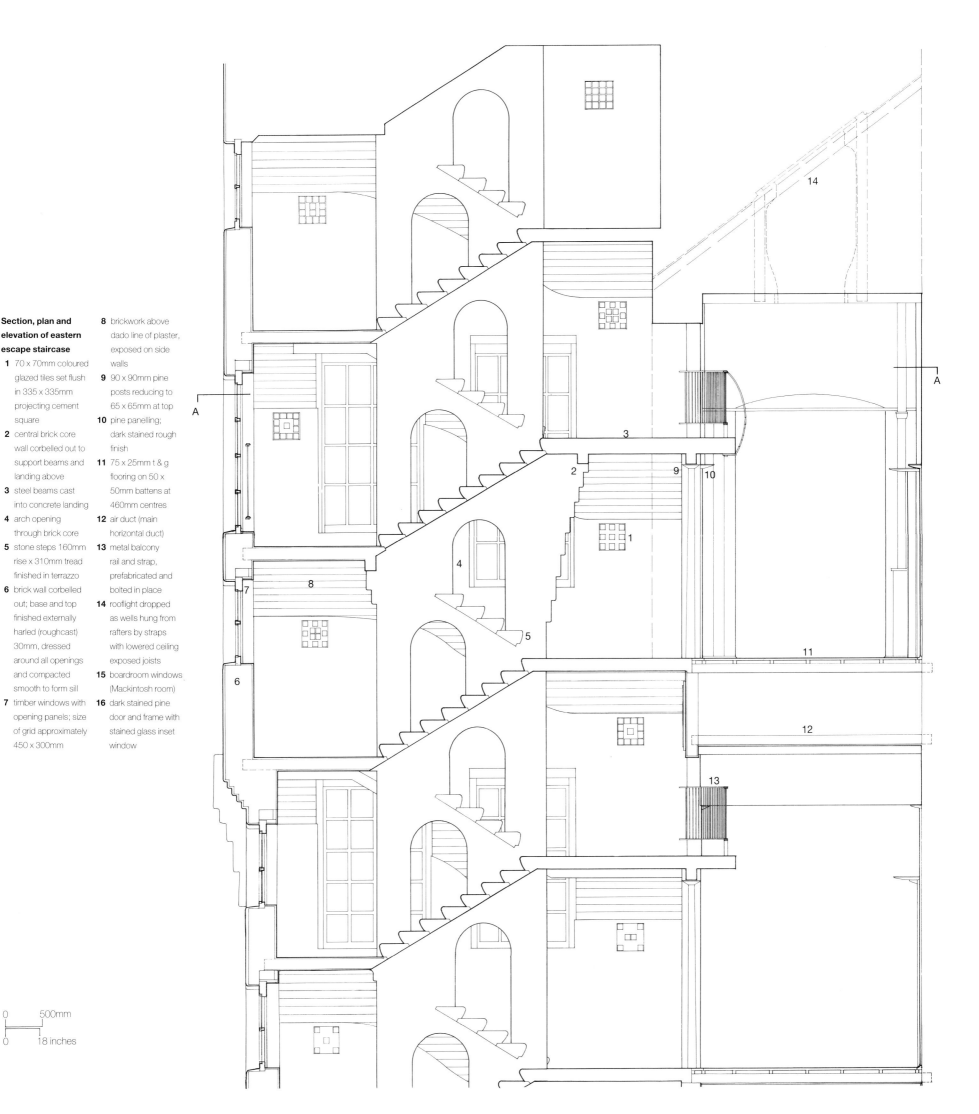

Section, plan and elevation of eastern escape staircase

1 70 x 70mm coloured glazed tiles set flush in 335 x 335mm projecting cement square

2 central brick core wall corbelled out to support beams and landing above

3 steel beams cast into concrete landing

4 arch opening through brick core

5 stone steps 160mm rise x 310mm tread finished in terrazzo

6 brick wall corbelled out; base and top finished externally harled (roughcast) 30mm, dressed around all openings and compacted smooth to form sill

7 timber windows with opening panels; size of grid approximately 450 x 300mm

8 brickwork above dado line of plaster, exposed on side walls

9 90 x 90mm pine posts reducing to 65 x 65mm at top

10 pine panelling; dark stained rough finish

11 75 x 25mm t & g flooring on 50 x 50mm battens at 460mm centres

12 air duct (main horizontal duct)

13 metal balcony rail and strap, prefabricated and bolted in place

14 rooflight dropped as wells hung from rafters by straps with lowered ceiling exposed joists

15 boardroom windows (Mackintosh room)

16 dark stained pine door and frame with stained glass inset window

0   500mm

0   18 inches

Library elevation, section and balcony details

1 580 x 200mm RSJ on stone and brick butts

2 50 x 13mm flat bar twisted straps held by riveted plates with 170 x 30mm diameter spacer bars; bolted through; straps riveted to RSJs supporting floor

3 floor grid exposed; upper RSJ in metal lath with plaster finish

4 window of roorn above with opening panel

5 RSJ encased in timber

6 balcony faced in alternating panels of 410 x 25mm and 520 x 25mm with carved panels over

7 doubie and single post columns pegged through and faced in 17mm board

8 100 x 100mm beam on steel T-beams built into brickwork to support balcony

9 ends of double balcony beams

10 framed storage and reading cupboards

11 storage cabinets following diagonals of window butts, with end support posts

12 full height metal window with six opening panels (1909)

13 built-in bookcases with leaded glass panels

14 balcony rail and posts

15 panel dropped to form pendant

16 3no 50 x 50mm posts between balcony facia and column, corners chamfered and painted in blue, green, red and white patterns

17 60 x 8mm plywood strip undulating between fixings

0　500mm

0　18 inches

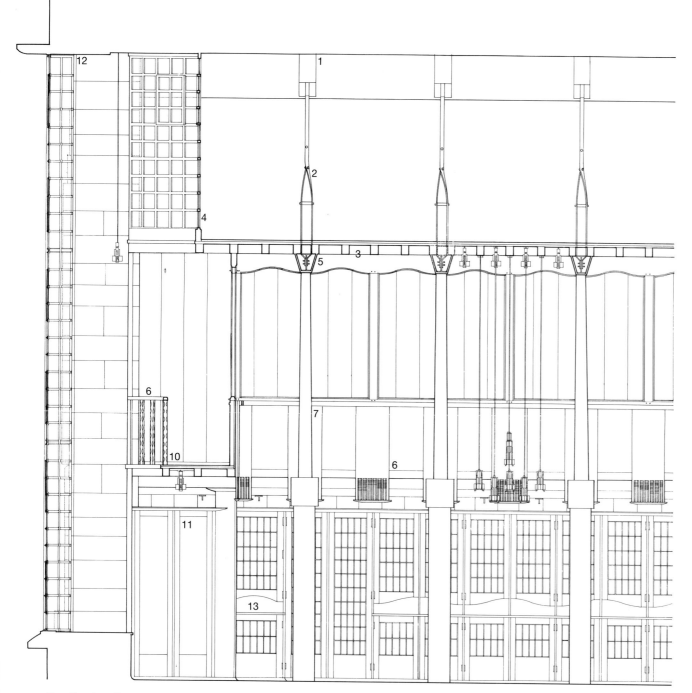

Elevational section

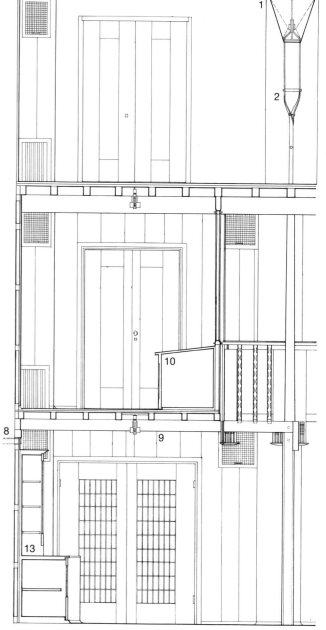

Section

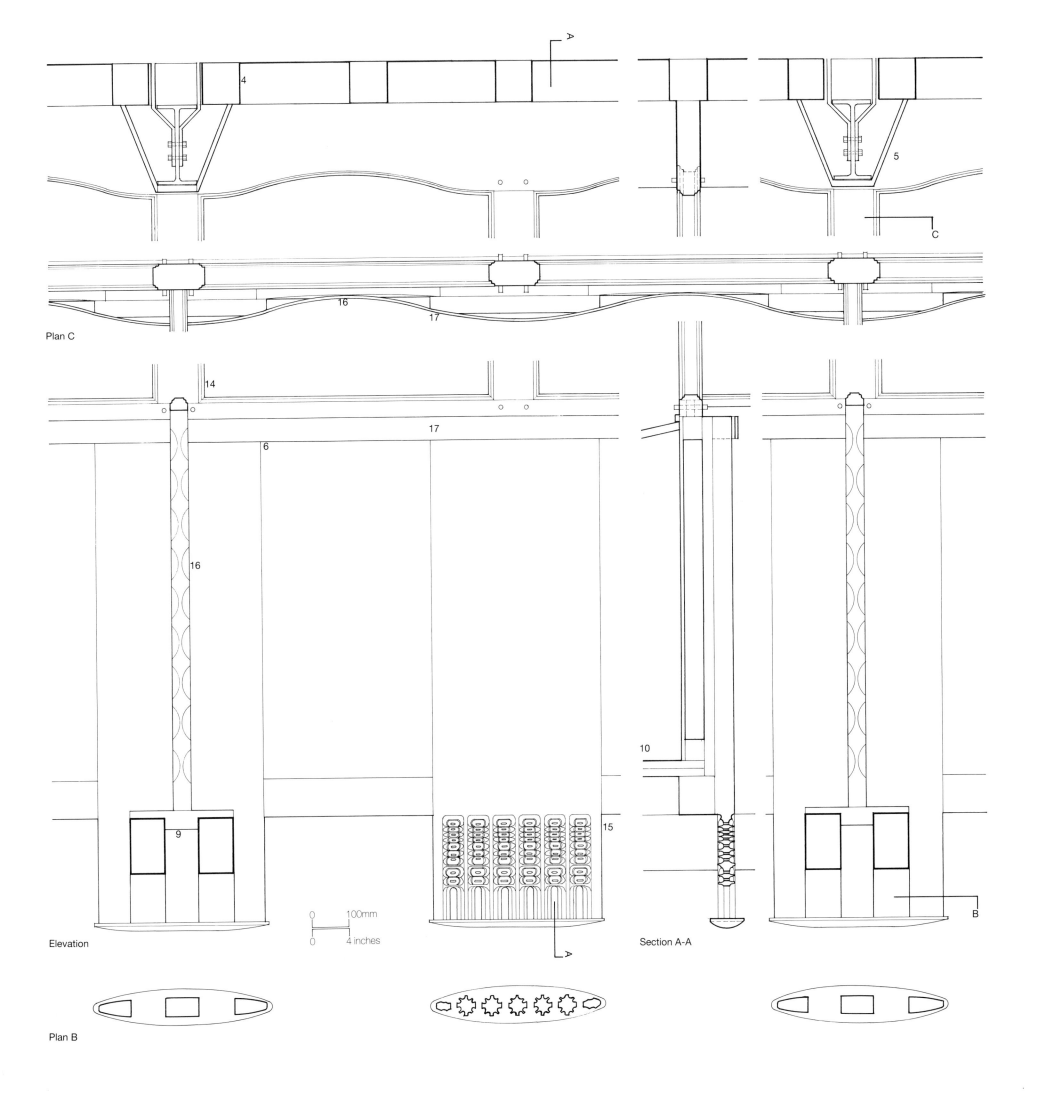

Plan C

Elevation

Plan B

Section A-A

0   100mm

0   4 inches

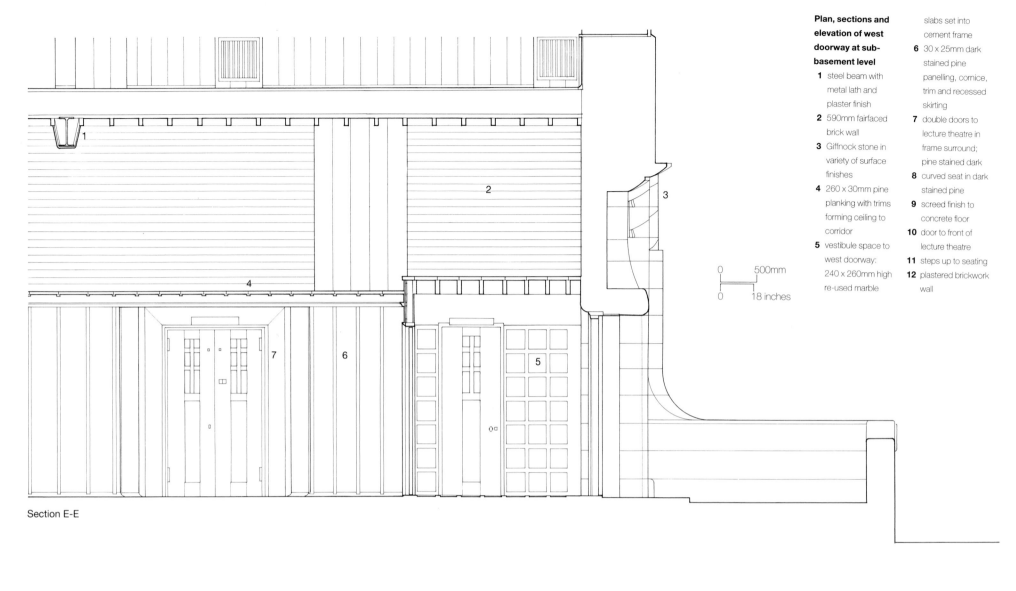

Section E-E

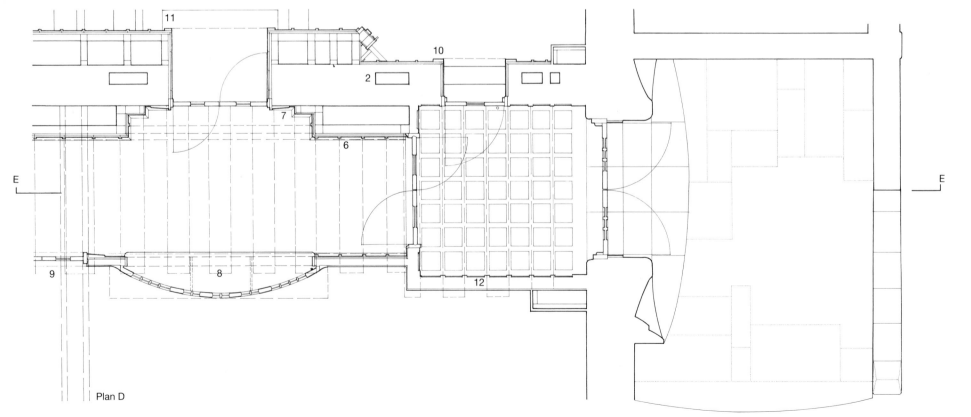

Plan D

Plan, sections and elevation of west doorway at sub-basement level

1 steel beam with metal lath and plaster finish
2 590mm fairfaced brick wall
3 Giffnock stone in variety of surface finishes
4 260 x 30mm pine planking with trims forming ceiling to corridor
5 vestibule space to west doorway: 240 x 260mm high re-used marble slabs set into cement frame
6 30 x 25mm dark stained pine panelling, cornice, trim and recessed skirting
7 double doors to lecture theatre in frame surround; pine stained dark
8 curved seat in dark stained pine
9 screed finish to concrete floor
10 door to front of lecture theatre
11 steps up to seating
12 plastered brickwork wall

0   500mm

0   18 inches

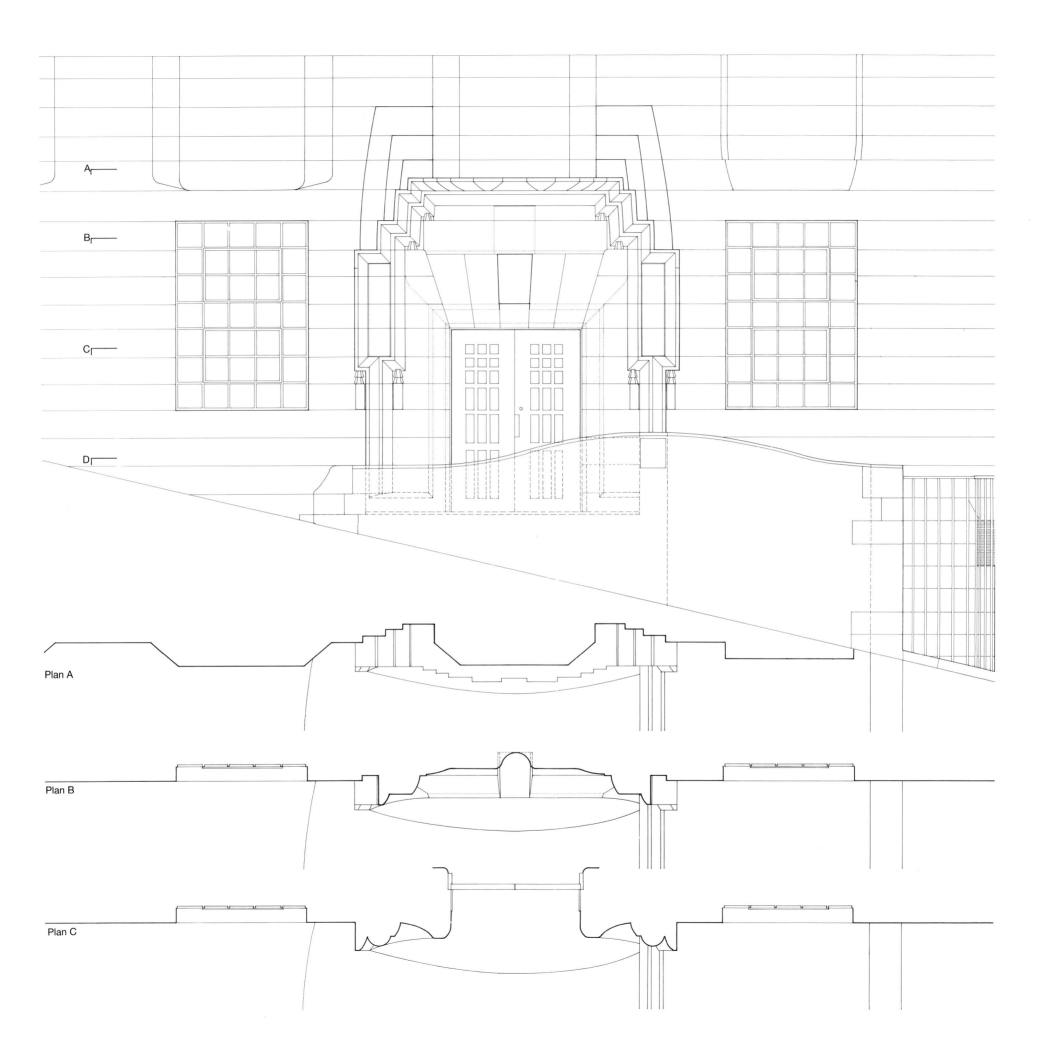

A

B

C

D

Plan A

Plan B

Plan C

Notes

1 Letter from Eyre Crome, ARA, Examiner from the Science and Art Department. Governors' Minutes, Glasgow School of Art, vol.2, 25 October 1882.

2 ibid, vol.2, 20 August 1884.

3 ibid, vol.3, 12 September 1892.

4 ibid, vol.3, quoting *Glasgow Herald*, 3 February 1893.

5 T. Howarth, *Charles Rennie Mackintosh and the Modern Movement*, pp.13–15.

6 Governors' Minutes, vol.2, 2 March 1885.

7 ibid, vol.2, 20 March, 24 April and 11 and 19 May 1885.

8 ibid, vol.2 quoting *Glasgow Herald* report, 16 October 1885.

9 ibid, vol.2, 22 December 1885.

10 ibid, vol.2, 2 April 1886.

11 ibid, vol.4, 16 May 1895.

12 ibid, vol.2, 10 December 1886; vol.3, 26 January 1888; 3 and 5 February 1889. Two letters from William Morris, dated 14 January and 6 February 1889 are among the GSA archives.

13 H. Muthesius, *The English House*, Crosby Lockwood Staples, 1979, p.51.

14 Governors' Minutes, vol.3, 22 September 1890.

15 The names of Herbert McNair and Frances Macdonald are among those members of staff complaining about the lack of a passenger lift. GSA archives, box B8/7.

16 A. Gomme and D. Walker, *The Architecture of Glasgow*, pp.172–73.

17 J. Honeyman, 'The Cathedral Church', *The Book of Glasgow Cathedral* (ed. G. Eyre-Todd), Monison Brothers, 1898.

18 Mackintosh Collection, Hunterian Art Gallery, University of Glasgow.

19 Governors' Minutes, vol.2, 30 November and 18 December 1882.

20 Howarth, op. cit., p.9.

21 Governors' Minutes, vol.3, 16 March 1894 to vol.4, 16 March 1896 *passim*.

22 'The Glasgow School of Art. Conditions of Competition', GSA archives.

23 Governors' Minutes, vol.4, 16 March 1896 to 13 January 1897.

24 GSA archives, letter book, 6 October 1910.

25 ibid. Box A/12, 'Description and Schedule of Contents'.

26 *Glasgow Herald* report contained in the Governors' Minutes, vol.4, 26 May 1898; 20 December 1899; 30 April 1900.

27 J.J. Burnet to W.F. Salmon, 19 January 1907. GSA archives, box A/7/2.

28 C.R. Mackintosh, 15 March 1907. GSA archives, letter book 1907–10.

29 P. Robertson (ed.), *Charles Rennie Mackintosh: The Architectural Papers*, p.52.

30 D. Brett, *C.R. Mackintosh: The Poetics of Workmanship*, Reaktion Books, 1992, p.77.

31 J. Macaulay, 'Elizabethan Architecture', *Charles Rennie Mackintosh: The Architectural Papers*, University of Glasgow Press, p.133.

32 J. Summerson, *The Turn of the Century: Architecture in Britain Around 1900*, Thames and Hudson, London, 1976, p.24; J. Summerson, *The Unromantic Castle*, Thames and Hudson, London, 1990, pp.235–44.

33 GSA archives, letter book 1907–10, 9 October 1907.

34 ibid, 5 February 1908.

35 Supra, n.22.

36 *A Guide to Crathes Castle and its Gardens*, The National Trust for Scotland, 1963, p.8, quoting Dr D. Simpson.

37 Robertson, op. cit., p.61.

38 ibid.

39 Ibid, p.134.

40 G. White, 'Some Glasgow Designers and their Work', *The Studio*, vol.II, p.29.

41 ibid, vol.XI, p.230.

42 ibid, vol.XI, p.237.

43 GSA archives, letter book, 21 October 1909.

44 W.R. Lethaby, *Architecture, Mysticism and Myth*, 1891 (republished 1974), Architectural Press, London, p.31.

45 *Glasgow Herald*, quoted by J. Dunlop, Mitchell Library, to W. Davidson, 20 April 1933. Mackintosh Collection, Hunterian Art Gallery, University of Glasgow.

46 C. Marriot, *Modern English Architecture*, 1924, p.129.

47 N. Pevsner, *C.R. Mackintosh*, Il Balcone, 1950.

Bibliography

Barnes, H.J., *Some Examples of Furniture by Charles Rennie Mackintosh in the Glasgow School of Art Collection*, Glasgow School of Art, Glasgow, 1969, revised 1978. The first review of Mackintosh's furniture and still invaluable despite the further addition of items to the collection.

Barnes, H.J., *Charles Rennie Mackintosh, Ironwork and Metalwork at Glasgow School of Art*, Glasgow School of Art, Glasgow, 1986, revised 1978. Like the above, this booklet consists mainly of a series of excellent photographs and line drawings and is the only study of Mackintosh's innovative use of iron.

Bilcliffe, R., *Charles Rennie Mackintosh: The Complete Furniture, Furniture Drawings, and Interior Designs*, Lutterworth Press, Guildford, 1979 and subsequent editions. A masterwork of scholarship bringing together material from many sources and an indispensable catalogue.

Bliss, D.P., *Charles Rennie Mackintosh and the Glasgow School of Art*, Glasgow School of Art, Glasgow, 1961, revised 1978. This is still one of the finest visual records of the building and is a useful record of both the building and its interiors before some recent changes were introduced.

Buchanan, W. (ed.), *Mackintosh's Masterwork: The Glasgow School of Art*, Richard Drew, Glasgow, 1989. Edited and produced by members of staff of the Glasgow School of Art, this is essential reading particularly as it includes for the first time details of the competition. The many illustrations are particularly memorable.

Gomme, A. and **Walker, D.**, *The Architecture of Glasgow*, Lund Humphries, London, 1968, reprinted 1987. Although much has been written about the architecture of the city in recent years nothing surpasses the wealth of scholarship found here. The first edition is a beautiful piece of book design.

Howarth, T., *Charles Rennie Mackintosh and the Modern Movement*, Routledge and Kegan Paul, London, 1952, second edition 1977. Despite the vast popular literature on Mackintosh, this remains the standard work for the range of scholarship which has not been reduced by recent archival discoveries and because the author was in Glasgow when many people who knew Mackintosh were still alive.

Macleod, R., *Charles Rennie Mackintosh*, Country Life Books, London, 1968. A good comprehensive account of Mackintosh's career which has stood the test of time. The book is especially useful for its analysis of current architectural theories at the turn of the century.

Nuttgens, P. (ed.), *Mackintosh and His Contemporaries in Europe and America*, John Murray, London, 1988. This is a series of papers delivered at the conference to mark the tenth anniversary of the founding of the Charles Rennie Mackintosh Society. It is unfortunate that the book is out of print since much of what is contained is not to be found elsewhere.

Pevsner, N., *Pioneers of the Modern Movement from William Morris to Walter Gropius*, Faber and Faber, London, 1936, revised 1960. This was the first account of Mackintosh and his place in the development of the modern movement.

Robertson, P. (ed.), *Charles Rennie Mackintosh: The Architectural Papers*, White Cockade Publishing, Wendelbury, 1990. It is doubtful if these juvenilia would have been published if they had been by anyone other than Mackintosh. That said, they do give insights into his reading and philosophy and are useful too for further study.

Walker, D.M., 'Charles Rennie Mackintosh', *Edwardian Architecture and its Origins* (ed. A. Service), Architectural Press, London, 1975. Lavishly illustrated, this is a comprehensive account of the main architectural movements and provides insight into Mackintosh's sources.

Chronology

1868 Charles Rennie Mackintosh is born in Glasgow, the son of a police superintendant

1882 The Lord Provost of Glasgow proposes that a new museum, art gallery and art school should be constructed on a site alongside the Corporation Galleries which housed the school of art

1883 Mackintosh enrols at the school of art as a part-time evening student

1884 Mackintosh begins a five-year architectural apprenticeship

1885 Francis Newbery is appointed head of the Glasgow School of Art

1889 Having completed his apprenticeship Mackintosh joins the firm of Honeyman and Keppie

1890 Drawings are prepared by Mackintosh, for an art gallery, concert hall and art school

1891 Having won the second Alexander Thomson Travelling Studentship, Mackintosh goes to Italy

1892 The South Kensington National Gold Medal is awarded to 'Chas R. McIntosh for Architecture'

1894 The governors of the school of art apply to the Bellahouston Trustees for a grant for a purpose-built art school

1895 The Bellahouston Trustees award £10,000 on condition that an equivalent sum is raised from other sources

1896 'A Limited Competition for the Proposed New School of Art' is announced. Eight Glasgow architectural firms are invited to participate, then the number is increased to 12 which includes Honeyman and Keppie

1897 On 13 January Honeyman and Keppie are selected as the winning firm

1898 Phase one of the new Glasgow School of Art commences. At the laying of the foundation stone Mackintosh is not among the platform party which includes John Honeyman and John Keppie

1899 Phase one is completed in December. At the opening ceremony Mackintosh is not included in the official platform party. John Keppie replies to the vote of thanks to the architects

1904 John Honeyman retires from his firm; Mackintosh becomes a partner. The firm is known as Honeyman, Keppie and Mackintosh

1907 Phase two of the Glasgow School of Art underway

1909 At the end of the year phase two is completed and Mackintosh is complimented publicly on the design

1910 A full set of drawings of the Glasgow School of Art as built is prepared by Honeyman, Keppie and Mackintosh

1913 Mackintosh resigns as a partner and soon leaves Glasgow for Walberswick, Suffolk, later moving to London before leaving Britain and settling at Port Vendres on the Mediterranean coast of France

1924 The first photograph is published of the completed Glasgow School of Art

1928 Mackintosh dies in London

1950 The first plan of the Glasgow School of Art is published

Bernard Maybeck
First Church of Christ, Scientist
Berkeley, California 1910

Edward R. Bosley

Photography
Peter Aprahamian; cover detail
also by Peter Aprahamian
Drawings
John Hewitt

Foreword

William Marquand
Emeryville, California

Called upon to build a church for a new sect [Maybeck] asked them about their beliefs, and was given testimony of such measureless confidence in their creed that he said it seemed a faith that had not been in the world since Christ was in the flesh. Then his problem, to him, was to design a church that would satisfy the joyous, holy feelings of an early Christian; perhaps an apostle. The result is a gilded, painted, grey and golden, blue and silver glory of Byzantine and Gothic elements that makes the heart sing to look at it.

Frank Morton Todd
Palace of Fine Arts and Lagoon
Paul Elder & Company
San Francisco, 1915

In common with other artists Virginia Woolf believed that the year 1910 brought a basic shift in human nature. Although we can see fundamental changes through generations of art, in retrospect we often remember only images of 'before' and 'after'. In works like First Church of Christ, Scientist, Berkeley, however, we see change at its vortex, a cohesive ensemble of ancient motifs and novel experimentation.

To Bernard Maybeck architecture is built art, and the ages of man's art manifest the whole of his being. While many architects of the new era would pursue a pared-down aesthetic of function, with the Christian Science church Maybeck provides a rare look inside the rich, expansive totality of man. Nested on a modest corner in Berkeley, its interior orchestrates aspects of our collective nature, offering such examples as the intimate sanctity of a Medieval chapel, the common-sense pragmatism of a modern factory, the thundering exuberance of Romantic opera, the rustic beauty of a fireside folk song. Virtually every ambience that Maybeck admired, including influences from Asia, takes part in this music, and does so with an honesty, unity, and beauty inspired, in part, by its patron.

In that sense the building was more than the work of a single creative talent. It was a collaboration with a congregation seeking a home. Edward Bosley's ground-breaking essay portrays the construction of the church as the unfolding of many unique aspirations and resources – it was the blossoming of an exotic flower.

Still, the church is thoroughly Maybeck and is widely regarded as his masterpiece. What was it, exactly, that would stir Maybeck's talents to full bloom?

Historically it is easy to classify Maybeck as a Romantic but this simply describes the wardrobe of what was an incredibly resilient self-styled artistic and spiritual identity. Uniquely, Maybeck proved impervious to the Age of Darwin marching alongside him, with its depiction of man as an aggressive bio-physical intellect. As brilliant as he could be, Maybeck felt that true creativity comes to a receptive heart, and is 'something no smart brain can figure out'. He often spoke of the marvellous inspiration he received as a youth in one of Paris's Medieval churches – to Maybeck, beauty is art's *summum bonum*, and it not only points to Beyond, it has its origins there.

To the Christian Scientists, this signified an essential truth. 'Spiritual sense', an idea with Puritan roots, was important to Mary Baker Eddy, the leader of the new movement. She taught that as we dwell on the things of God, Spirit, patterns of divine perfection begin to emerge in our own expression and experience.

The affinity that developed between the congregation and Maybeck was, however, more than spiritual. A prominent Episcopalian observed that Christian Science reawakened the world to the *workable* nature of Christianity. Members see it as the 'reinstatement of primitive Christianity and its lost element of healing'. Christian Scientists see Jesus' life as 'divinely natural', a healing life that was rooted in the here and now. One's spiritual life today, they insist, can have the same roots and the same useful, redeeming influence.

Maybeck marvelled at the sincerity of these claims. Like the angel in Wim Wenders's *Wings of Desire* Maybeck was 'spiritual', yet this son of a cabinet-maker, at home in the aroma of sawdust, yearned for an art 'rooted in the real, the practical, the utilitarian'. He took the commission with great anticipation and developed an abiding interest in this 'new-old' Scriptural teaching.

As for the Christian Scientists, their architecture was normally a customized Puritan meeting house, Byzantine dome, etc. In Berkeley, however, they sought a structure of the primal. They told Maybeck that foremost in his thought must be pure, divine qualities. The lives of early Christians shined with the beauty and power of God. These qualities, they reasoned, were just as available today.

This bond of hearts, minds, and aspirations proved special. The trust that the congregation placed in their architect became, in Maybeck's own heart, a simple confidence that God would work through his work. The results made him proud. His church hints, unlike any other building I am aware of, at the coherent whole of what we are.

2

3

A touchstone of romanticized architecture, First Church of Christ, Scientist in Berkeley, California has stood, since 1910, as a paradigm of enigmatic beauty. Its eclectic and inventive design derives from Byzantine, Romanesque and Gothic traditions, but the date of construction and straightforward use of materials cast the church within the bounds of the American Arts and Crafts idiom. Its layered, complex exterior and bold structural system shun ecclesiastical norms, yet both are indispensable to the dynamism and intimacy of the dramatic auditorium, a space of worship which is so completely reassuring and right. It challenges attempts at categorization, but the ensemble of forms and forces at work has been so thoughtfully directed, skilfully proportioned, and beautifully detailed in the hands of the architect, Bernard Maybeck, that we revere the church today as a courageous and sublime building achievement.

Roots among old-world artisans

The legacy of Bernard Maybeck occupies an obscure niche in the history of American architecture, one which reflects his artistic, imaginative and idiosyncratic personality. Bernard Ralph Maybeck (1862–1957) was born into a family which hoped to raise him for artistic pursuits. His father, Bernhardt Maybeck, emigrated from his native Germany with his brother, Henry, to take advantage of the comparatively greater political and intellectual freedom of America after revolutionary upheavals swept Europe in 1848.[1] The two brothers apprenticed to a Staten Island cabinet-maker, learning traditional European wood carving. Bernhardt met and married a fellow expatriate, Elisa Kern, and the two settled in Manhattan's Greenwich Village. Not far from their home, Bernhardt opened a cabinet shop specializing in bench-made furniture. Here, he exploited his carving talent while his partner, Joseph Reinal, executed joinery for their commissions. Work progressed well, and at home the birth of the Maybecks' son Bernard completed a happy domestic picture. Elisa died in 1865 when Ben (as Bernard came to be called) was only three. Despite Ben's youth, his mother had left him with a clear memory of her urging him to become an artist. His father was similarly inclined, encouraging his son to spend his evenings drawing.[2] Now a widower, Bernhardt left the cabinet-making partnership to join Pottier and Stymus, a large architectural carving and custom furniture firm, where he became foreman of carving.

As young Ben grew from childhood into adolescence he made satisfactory progress at school, but later at the College of the City of New York he ran into difficulties when confronted with the repetitive aspects of chemistry coursework. Probably sensing that his true calling would be outside the sciences, Maybeck left school to join his father at Pottier and Stymus where he apprenticed by running errands and tracing the occasional shop drawing of Pullman Parlor Cars, a major client.[3] Ben adjusted haltingly to the hierarchy and pressure of a commercial enterprise but developed confidence in his nascent drawing ability while designing an ingenious reversible Pullman seat. Believing that his real talent might lie in design, Bernhardt arranged for Ben to sail from New York in 1881 to take a position in the firm's Paris studio.

The Paris office of Pottier and Stymus was located in the Latin Quarter, not far from the Ecole des Beaux-Arts, the most respected academic institution of the day to train professional architects. Maybeck soon became attracted by the stylish appearance of the architecture students he saw in the boulevards. Recalling the elegant figure of an architect he had once seen in 'kid gloves and a pot hat', he believed that this profession would be his true destiny. With perhaps little notion of what the study of architecture at the prestigious Ecole des Beaux-Arts actually entailed, he sat the rigorous entrance examination and qualified, coming 22nd among the 250 applicants.[4]

A Classicist's training, a Medievalist's wanderings

At the Ecole, Maybeck was indoctrinated in the prevailing architectural tradition whose curriculum focused on a building's composition and character, stressing the grandeur of historical styles. The traditional emphasis at the Ecole had formerly disallowed the tenets espoused by John Ruskin and Eugène Emmanuel Viollet-le-Duc which championed the inherent value of craftsmanship and the natural expression of materials and functional expression of structure. Instead of the temples of ancient Greece and Rome, Ruskin and Viollet cited as their paradigm the Gothic cathedrals and their artisan-

builders. Indeed, Viollet-le-Duc had taught non-Classicist ideals at the Ecole and was dismissed for this reason in 1867. By the time Maybeck had arrived, however, Viollet's concepts had been somewhat rehabilitated, enough to generate in Maybeck at least a long-lasting reverence for Medieval architecture. He recalled being taught that the plan of a building should generate its overall organization and aspect, and that the character of its elevations should reflect its intended use. Specifically, he was told that ' ... anyone can make elevations, but the plan is the backbone of anything beautiful'. This was more progressive than the Classicist line of thinking, and it was a useful concept, especially since Maybeck believed that 'beauty is the essence of architecture'.[5]

Maybeck received a sound training at the Ecole, but he wisely tempered it with his own investigations. He travelled to the cathedrals of the region, sketching and seeking inspiration at first hand. To his credit, he left Europe having sought as much from extra-curricular visits to Gothic and Romanesque churches as he had gained in the ateliers and classrooms of his formal instruction.

4

5

Professional beginnings and influences

Returning to New York in 1886, Maybeck
found work with Thomas Hastings, a friend
from the Ecole, who, with John Carrère
(another Ecole student), had recently left
the renowned firm of McKim Mead and
White to form their own, Carrère and
Hastings. Their first commission was for
a large resort hotel, the Ponce de Leon in
St Augustine, Florida. Construction was
already in progress when Maybeck joined
the firm, but working on the Ponce de Leon
and its sister hotel, the Alcazar, gave him
a chance to test both his formal and
informal European education.[6]

After leaving the east for a brief period
of work in Kansas City (where he met his
future wife, Annie White), Maybeck travelled
to California in 1890. This move was
prompted by encouraging reports of work
to be had coming from Willis Polk, another
young architect who had moved to San
Francisco from New York and whose family
Maybeck had also become acquainted with
in Kansas City. Maybeck may also have
chosen San Francisco to be closer to
his cousin, the son of his father's brother,
Henry.[7] Taking on a brief assignment with
the firm of Wright and Sanders, Maybeck
spent part of 1890 in Salt Lake City and
returned to Kansas City in October to
marry Annie White. The two moved west
together late that year to set up their
household in Oakland, near the eastern
shore of San Francisco Bay.

An excellent draughtsman, Maybeck
soon found employment, though not in
an architect's office but with the Charles
M Plum Company, interior designers and
makers of custom furniture. Maybeck had
been promised work, however, by the
architect A Page Brown (1859–96), who
had also recently come from New York.
Brown operated a successful firm which
included Willis Polk (1867–1924) and
A C Schweinfurth (1864–1900), both of
whom had worked for him in New York,
coincidentally in the same building
occupied by Maybeck's former employer
Carrère and Hastings. The promised job
with A Page Brown did not materialize until
two years later, causing Maybeck to remain
with the Plum Company longer than he
might have preferred. Once in Brown's
office, however, he was back in his element.
He assisted A C Schweinfurth, Brown's
chief designer, with the competition for
the California Building at the World's
Columbian Exposition in Chicago, and
the Brown plan, including detailing by
Maybeck, was ultimately chosen to
represent the state at the fair in 1893.
Its romantic references to the Franciscan
missions of early California reflected a
prevailing stylistic choice among California
architects, but the dome, part of Maybeck's
contribution, was heralded as innovative
and promising. Maybeck was appointed
construction supervisor in Chicago,
a position that afforded him ample
opportunity to scrutinize the highly-popular
Exposition first-hand. The vast scale and
romantic pomp of the main buildings,
dubbed the 'White City', appealed to his
Beaux-Arts roots, but Maybeck's active
imagination and intellect retained an equal
reverence for the romantic and anonymous
Gothic builders, the craftsmen whose
legacy was to play a key role in his future.

Following the Chicago Exposition, a formative collaboration for Maybeck was undoubtedly the commission which Brown had received to design the San Francisco Swedenborgian Church in 1894. While the extent of Maybeck's involvement in the rustic Swedenborgian project is undocumented, he is likely to have contributed to it, probably in decorative detailing, since A C Schweinfurth had primary design responsibility in Brown's office.[8] Through mutual friends, Maybeck knew the Swedenborgian Church client, the Reverend Joseph Worcester (himself an amateur architect), and admired the unpainted, wood-shingled home the minister had created for himself in 1876, long before the style became widely accepted.[9] Worcester's well-reasoned design concept for the church would have appealed strongly to Maybeck since it required taking unusual steps to reflect the natural surroundings, both in structure and materials. The most visible manifestation of Worcester's philosophy of building was the remarkable truss and knee-brace system which employed California madrone trees, exposed and with the bark left on. The resulting structure, and the nature-based design philosophy espoused by its influential pastor, were to become cornerstones of the Arts and Crafts movement in California.[10]

An individualist emerges in the 'Athens of the Pacific'

Despite his early experience designing public buildings, and a reputation which now rests on non-residential architecture (First Church of Christ, Scientist and the 1915 Palace of Fine Arts), Maybeck's early practice involved a significant amount of domestic architecture. After 1908, he designed several homes for wealthy clients in San Francisco, but his signature innovations were more persuasively developed in the earlier homes he had designed for upper-middle-class clients in the hills of the university town of Berkeley, across the bay. Berkeley's intelligentsia provided a congenial and fertile field for innovative architecture. Berkeley also offered the attraction of a somewhat sunnier climate than San Francisco, as well as spectacular topography near the shore of San Francisco Bay. Situated on a natural slope descending west, facing the dramatic isthmus of the Golden Gate, Berkeley was a quiet suburb of 13,000 at the turn of the twentieth century. It was a pastoral place well-suited to raising families in a setting close to nature, higher education and commerce. Maybeck's design and drafting

6

7

8 Mary Baker Eddy, Founder of
The First Church of Christ,
Scientist.
9 The First Church of Christ,
Scientist: The Mother Church in
Boston, Massachusetts, 1894.
The larger Renaissance revival
extension was completed
in 1904.

8

talents, combined with his own romantic vision for the community's hillside neighbourhoods, were suited to the spirit of what became known as the 'Athens of the Pacific'.[11]

An important aesthetic collaboration and long-lasting friendship developed in 1891 between Maybeck and a young Berkeley poet, Charles Keeler. They met by chance, but partly because Keeler and Maybeck both stood out in their dress and demeanour. Keeler described sighting Maybeck in his Bohemian garb on the San Francisco ferry and compared it with his own affected style: 'Instead of a vest he wore a sash, and his suit seemed like homespun of a dark brown color … Perhaps we were both sufficiently unusual in appearance to attract one another. In those days I used to wear an old-fashioned broadcloth cape … [and] carried [a] gold-headed cane'.[12] The two men became friends. A sensitive and creative individual, Keeler was drawn to Maybeck's artistic opinions and became his first residential client in 1895. Both were later to become the primary proponents of Berkeley's artistic and rustic life-style.

A group of concerned and design-minded citizens was organized in 1898 as the Hillside Club. Its goal was to promote the ideals of a simple home life characterized by unpainted, shingle-clad houses surrounded by regionally-appropriate and sensitively-designed landscaping. Maybeck and Keeler figured prominently in this cause. During the first decade of the new century, when Berkeley's population more than trebled to 40,000, Hillside Club members reasoned that it was crucial in maintaining Berkeley's character that they promote the awareness of good design tenets during the inevitable building boom which would accompany rapid growth. Keeler's important 1904 essay, *The Simple Home*, gave voice to Maybeck's philosophies of design and became a virtual code, graciously imposed on the property owners and home builders of the Berkeley hills. It became the manifesto of the club – an appealing treatise on proper Berkeley hill life. In it, Keeler held forth on the virtues of simplicity, and illustrated his prose with photographs of Maybeck's houses, among others. Keeler wrote: 'In the Simple Home all is quiet in effect, restrained in tone, yet natural and joyous in its frank use of unadorned material. Harmony of line and balance of proportion is not obscured by meaningless ornamentation; harmony of color is not marred by violent contrasts. Much of the construction shows, and therefore good workmanship is required and the craft of the carpenter is restored to its old-time dignity'.[13] These words could have been (and probably were, at one time or another) intoned by Maybeck himself.

Maybeck's domestic architectural practice began to take root and flourish. Notoriety came not only from his distinctive manner of home-building – inventive floor

plans, interiors of unpainted redwood, exteriors of unpretentious wood shingles – but also from his high-profile connection with the driving force in Berkeley, the University of California. Phoebe Apperson Hearst, philanthropic widow of mining millionaire Senator George Hearst, had acted on a suggestion from Maybeck to sponsor an international competition to design a master plan for the university. In 1896, at the age of 34, Maybeck was put in charge of administering the competition and establishing guidelines. He travelled with Annie throughout Europe to consult with jurors, and with Mrs Hearst attended the judging of the first round of submissions. Maybeck's important role in the competition, while it brought the criticism inevitable to such projects, also helped him gain invaluable experience as well as a reputation for having a strong architectural vision. The competition absorbed Maybeck's attention for several years and kept his name and achievements in the public eye. During the decade following the conclusion of the university competition, Maybeck grew to the height of his creative powers, undertaking nearly a hundred design projects of one kind or another over the ten-year period. It was during this busy period of his career, at the age of 47, that Maybeck was presented with the opportunity to design his masterpiece, First Church of Christ, Scientist, Berkeley.

A young and pioneering church

The Christian Science faith was relatively new, having been formally founded in New England by Mary Baker Eddy in 1879. Loosely associated with late-nineteenth-century alternative religious movements, the church enjoyed steady growth despite its unorthodox teachings, especially those regarding healing outside the mainstream medical profession. Christian Science churches held primarily to prevailing architectural forms, especially Classic and Renaissance revivals which had been popularized at the Chicago Exposition in 1893. Perhaps because its teachings were unfamiliar and often criticized by the uninitiated, most branch churches may have sought to minimize the attention paid to them through largely non-controversial and even unremarkable architecture. Mrs Eddy's teachings on the building of new structures emphasizes spirituality and calls for little fanfare: 'No large gathering of people nor display shall be allowed when laying the Corner Stone of a Church of Christ, Scientist. Let the ceremony be devout. No special trowel should be used'.[14] Mrs Eddy did not elaborate on what an ideal church edifice should look like. The First Church of Christ, Scientist in Boston, Massachusetts, known as The Mother Church, combined its original Richardson-inspired structure (1893–4) with an imposing extension of Renaissance revival design completed in 1904. When a branch church desired to erect a new building, there were few stylistic guidelines beyond the diversity of existing Christian Science structures.

Berkeley members organize and purchase land

In Berkeley, the Christian Science Church was formed officially in 1905 as an offshoot of a larger church in neighbouring Oakland. Informal meetings had taken place in homes and meeting halls since 1897. Immediately after the official organization of the Berkeley church the Board of Directors (now Executive Board) appointed a 'committee on the selection of a lot for building'.[15] Several parcels were considered, including a building site at the intersection of Dwight Way and Bowditch Street. An option was also proposed to 'buy the Congregational Church and move it to another lot ... offered for $7,000'. This idea was apparently of scant interest, since the next entry in the minutes returns to the subject of the corner lot at Dwight and Bowditch. The actual purchase of the property proceeded rather unsteadily at first. The original offering price was recorded in the minutes of 31 March 1905 as $7,500 for the 100 x 150ft lot, or $6,000 for a smaller 100 x 100ft sub-division on the same parcel of land. In May, the committee reported that their offer of $7,250 for the entire lot had been declined, and that the asking price of $7,500 had been re-confirmed. By the June 1st meeting, however, the asking price for the large lot had risen to $8,000. No discussion regarding the price discrepancy was recorded in the minutes, but in an effort to secure the figure from further fluctuation, and in an impressive show of support for the whole endeavour, the assembled directors personally pledged sufficient gifts and loans to secure the purchase of the land.[16]

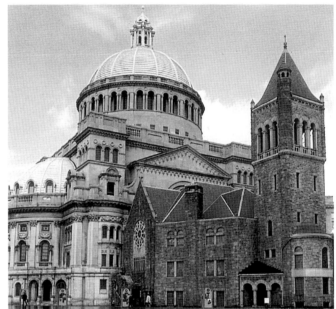

9

10 Julia Morgan, St John's Presbyterian Church, Berkeley, 1908–10. While the exterior has a dignified, if domestic, scale, the interior recalls a vernacular barn with its simple, exposed trusses.

Over the next few years, as church membership grew, funds were raised for a building. On 22 October 1908, a meeting of the board of directors convened to appoint a committee to investigate and propose a new church building. At a full membership meeting in November, a vote was even taken on the building material they would prefer: 21 voted in favour of wood, 50 for stone. A minimum budget of $25,000 was set, with no upward limit.

10

The search for an architect

In August of 1909, the newly-formed Plans Committee made up of five women, met to consider hiring an architect, a charge given to them by the 25-member Building Committee. Notes recorded later by Plans Committee chairwoman, Eulora Jennings, state: 'it was the opinion of all of the members ... that it would be desirable to have some plans by prominent architects ...'.[17] She reported that among others, the Plans Committee visited St John's Church, a dramatic wooden hall designed for the Presbyterian Church by Julia Morgan in 1908. Morgan was a gifted protégée of Maybeck's, and with his help in the late-1890s became the first woman ever admitted to the Ecole des Beaux-Arts.[18] Eulora Jennings noted that St John's Church 'cost about $6,000 and seats five hundred'. As they visited the church, the committee would have had to visualize what Morgan might do with a budget more than four times greater. The notes make no mention of Morgan (or Maybeck) by name, but state that the same day, after the St John's visit, a 'committee of three' went to San Francisco to 'interview the architects'. One had apparently moved and could not be found. Jennings writes: 'The others both said substantially the same thing, that it was not customary with them to submit plans – that this was very

unsatisfactory both to them and would be so to us, and that the thing for us to do was to settle upon one architect and then have him work out what we wanted'.[19] It is a matter of speculation that Maybeck himself might have been the one who provided this bit of advice, but the committee was ultimately persuaded to accept it.

No judgements, good or bad, were recorded regarding any of the buildings or architects the Plans Committee visited that day. According to his own account, Maybeck initially declined the invitation to design the church, but during a second visit from the committee – this time with all five members in attendance – he became convinced (and possibly flattered), that the women were serious and sincere in their desire to hire him. At the first meeting he recalled telling the committee that: 'it couldn't be done', probably referring to the committee's clear notion of what they wanted and Maybeck's doubt that their vision might coincide with his. At the second meeting he softened, recalling that 'they consulted God before they came to see their architect – they told me so ... And then I made up my mind that since they were so very sincere about it there must be something to it. And since that time, I believe that God had all to do with it'.[20]

One gets the impression from the accumulated evidence, especially a noticeable lack of broad debate over the selection of an architect, that the committee may have been adopted by Maybeck nearly as much as he was by them. His gentle and thoughtful personality and even his artistic manner of dress must have made a persuasive impression on the committee. They were familiar with his work living among his ubiquitous shingled designs in the Berkeley hills and at least one member of the larger Building

Committee, John Gilson Howell, had close contact with Maybeck's work.[21] Before opening his own antiquarian bookshop in 1912, Howell worked for Paul Elder in the San Francisco shop which bore his name. In 1906, Maybeck designed a temporary replacement for the shop, which had been destroyed in the city's disastrous earthquake and fire, and in 1908 designed its permanent interior in an existing building. It is worth noting that Maybeck's decorative use of Gothic tracery in the Paul Elder Shop is nearly identical to much of what he designed later in First Church of Christ, Scientist. Paul Elder's parents, Scott and Mary Elder, were also both active in the church. Mary became a member of the Building Committee in March 1911 when construction was under way.[22]

The Plans Committee's final report on the search for an architect was made to the larger Building Committee on 27 September 1909, concluding: '[The] committee has considered some five or six sets of plans that have been submitted and have also considered some twelve or thirteen architects. We have made visits to several of these. We unanimously report that in our opinion Mr Maybeck would understand best what our wants are and is best qualified to express them in this building. It is from our talks with him that many of the ideas expressed in the foregoing recommendations have originated. We are not to present any plans to him, but give him simply this statement of our needs & allow him to work out the building with this as a basis'.[23] The trust inherent in this statement is revealing. The committee, headed by an artist, Eulora Jennings, was deeply respectful of the need to allow another artist's vision to evolve, without holding it blindly to strict dictates. This may have grated on a membership which had gone so far as to vote on the material to be used in construction. The closing sentences of the Plans Committee report hint of tension and even defensiveness about the selection process, unintentionally confirming that Maybeck may have been the only one the committee had seriously considered: 'We shall be glad to inform any of the committee as to what architects we have considered. It is hardly necessary to bespeak your cordial and loyal support of the one that has been chosen'. Some members of the Building Committee had obviously disapproved of the eccentric Maybeck or felt that the Plans Committee had acted hastily in selecting an architect.[24] But when it came to a vote, the committee's recommendation to retain Mr Maybeck was adopted by the 25-member Building Committee.

11

12

13

11, 12, 13 Bernard Maybeck, Paul Elder bookshop, San Francisco, 1908, interior details (now demolished).

14 First Church of Christ
Scientist, Berkeley. Maybeck's
presentation rendering of interior
looking northeast. A number
of details shown here were
included in the finished
auditorium.

15 Following the original
landscape plan, wisteria partially
obscures the west tracery
window of the church, bringing
nature closer to the interior.

An early Christian vision for the church

When asked to remember how he conceived the design of the church, Maybeck recalled late in his life that his sense of the committee's sincerity reminded him of the early Christians. This would have been appreciated by his clients as a positive sign, since their founder, Mrs Eddy, had sought to 'establish a church ... which should reinstate primitive Christianity and its lost element of healing'. An endearing quirk was Maybeck's tendency to categorize his clients according to the historical era he believed befitted them. He implied that he had assigned the Medieval Romanesque period to the devout committee of Christian Scientists, possibly because of their founder's well-known quest to rehabilitate ancient aspects of Christian faith.[25] In particular, Maybeck related that he began the design process for the church by contemplating what a twelfth-century builder would do with such a commission. In a partial flight of hyperbole, he described the final product as '... pure Romanesque made out of modern materials', confirming that his intention had been to develop the Medieval theme.[26]

The design programme

The programme to guide the design of the church was recorded in a 14-page handwritten recommendation, a thoughtful and thorough instruction covering all aspects of the church edifice from the character of the building to the provision of space for the heating and ventilation equipment. It opens with the charge that: 'The Church should be a perfect concept of mental architectural skill, manifesting unity, harmony, beauty, light and peace. A structure denoting progress in all lines and strictly individual in character, designed to meet our present needs and in keeping with the artistic surroundings. It should express simplicity and beauty'. A quote from Mary Baker Eddy was also included in the document and may have struck a sympathetic chord with Maybeck: 'Mrs Eddy says ... "Beauty is a thing of life which dwells forever in the eternal Mind and reflects the charms of His goodness in expression, form, outline, and color"'. In closing, the programme credits Maybeck's help in developing the goals in consultation with the committee, further suggesting that he was a clear, and perhaps early, favourite in the selection process.[27]

14

A design of few compromises

The first official conceptualization of the church on paper was a series of coloured sketches which Maybeck presented with his interpretation to the Building Committee at a meeting on 17 January 1910. The Plans Committee warned the larger committee in their written report: 'Mr Maybeck ... expressed a wish to have the Building Committee fully apprised of the scheme for a building which he had in mind, stating that it was somewhat unusual and he did not wish to have any surprises confront the committee later on'. The coloured sketches depict a church so similar to what was actually built, that they stand as persuasive evidence that Maybeck was in firm control of his clients' hearts and minds from the beginning of the design process. Among the surviving preliminary coloured renderings by Maybeck, the primary axis-of-entry side, the south elevation, shows an east–west pergola and trellis structure interrupted by an entry gate of Gothic tracery design, separating the portico from the street.[28] Above and behind the main portico looms the high, shadowy form of the main roof, its gable hidden by deeply projecting eaves. Left of the portico, a pergola structure is supported by fluted concrete columns topped with decorated capitals in a geometric theme. The pergola's columns, as well as the trellis columns east of the portico, is depicted almost to resemble the remains of an ancient temple. They seem separate from the main building and give the appearance of a romantic ruin, complete with encroaching vegetation. Behind the columns, the core building appears, looking more complete and intact, as if it had been built centuries later.

A second exterior sketch, a pastel, is a perspective taken from the west elevation looking north along Bowditch Street. Wisteria vines are shown as mature plantings, entwined amid the concrete pillars. A third sketch shows the rich interior detail Maybeck envisioned, much of which remarkably survived committee reviews and inevitable budget adjustments. But perhaps the greatest tribute to Maybeck's power of architectural vision is how accurately the rendering communicates the Medieval mood of the main auditorium space as it was built. Maybeck's signature Gothic tracery panels in the sketch are remarkably similar to those finally installed, and the colours chosen to enliven the concrete piers in the preliminary drawing are of the same palette as those ultimately used.

15

18

19

16 West elevation taken from the southwest corner of Dwight Way and Bowditch Street, c1911.

17 West elevation, c1913. Photo taken from northwest, opposite property line on Bowditch Street. Note the 'well-head' design of ventilation outlet surmounted by a planter box and pitched roof.

18 East window. Maybeck's interpretation of Gothic tracery is carried out in concrete on pre-fabricated steel armatures. Here and throughout the church decorative complexity increases from bottom to top.

19 Music cabinet, designed by Maybeck, is flanked by industrial sash in west end of narthex.

Construction and occupancy

Maybeck's sketches were approved at the next meeting of the Building Committee and exhibited for the review of church members. For this purpose, a room in a local bank building was rented and staffed for one week by committee members who were appointed to explain the drawings. This phase of scrutiny passed with no objections being brought at the full membership meeting on the 5th of February, and on the 28th Maybeck was asked to 'proceed with greatest possible rapidity to complete the details of the plans'.[29] These were completed in Maybeck's office, and included small changes and additions voted for by the committee. In June, Charles F Wieland, church member and chair of the Construction Committee, was formally engaged as Supervisor of Construction to act in the capacity of general contractor. Low bidder William L Boldt was chosen as primary building contractor in August and a building permit was issued on 26 September 1910, nearly one year to the day after the Building Committee had approved the selection of Bernard Maybeck as architect.

The construction and furnishing of the church was an elaborate committee endeavour for the church membership. Sub-committees had been established from the 25 members of the Building Committee to oversee separately general construction, landscaping and grounds, furnishings, the pipe organ and finances. Despite the seeming obstacle of involving so many committees and individuals, a relative working harmony and rhythm seems to have been achieved. The building was ready to occupy for services on Wednesday evening, 16 August 1911, less than a year after construction had begun.[30]

Exterior forms of truth and beauty

The finished product of First Church of Christ, Scientist, Berkeley surpassed the expectations of its delighted members. In an interview some years later, one member remarked: 'We wanted a church by Mr Maybeck … but we never dreamed of such a beautiful thing'.[31] Maybeck had promised a 'somewhat unusual' structure, but also said he would pursue a truthful use of materials. Both sentiments reflected his natural inclination to search for beauty in his designs.[32]

Seen from the street, the exterior forms seem kinetic. The eye is drawn briskly from one form to the next, from the stepped and separated masses of the concrete planting boxes at the foundation level to the hyperactive interplay of surface planes and roof-lines, and the intricately articulated pergola and trellis structures. But visually colliding elements of the composition also alternate with more serene, comforting signals of vernacular domestic architecture – the low angle of the roofs, heavy wood posts, exposed beam ends and rafters – all an elaboration of the Craftsman idiom. The only overt ecclesiastical references are the exquisite Gothic tracery windows which punctuate three elevations. Despite a profusion of elements which might have conflicted, with potentially unfortunate results in less sensitive hands, Maybeck managed to finesse it all, blending diversity with grace and dignity to earn an awed respect.

Materials used on the exterior range from the mundane to the curious. Simple concrete, reinforced and poured into

16

17

20

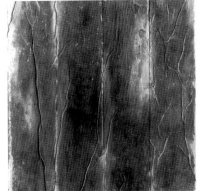

21

board forms, predominates on the ground level. Industrial sash windows, not unprecedented but certainly atypical in a church project, were supplied under modest protest from the fabricator. In refusing to reply to the architect's initial request for a bid, the Detroit Steel Products Company elicited this frustrated response from Maybeck's office: '... you say you do not recommend [industrial steel sash] for use in churches. You of course do not understand the nature of the work in which we wish to use them ... and will again ask you to kindly quote us on [them] ...'.[33] The sash was ultimately produced by the reluctant supplier. It was then installed and glazed with 'antique clear glass'. During the glazing process, the panes were bisected by vertical leading to give a lighter, more delicate appearance to the windows.

An asbestos insulation material, 'asbestos lumber', was specified for exterior walls in areas not filled with steel sash or board and batten panelling. These inexpensive asbestos panels were also highly improbable for use on a church exterior, but they nonetheless approximate the colour of the concrete used on the ground level, promoting a thorough visual unity. The panels are enlivened by Maybeck's clever use of small red squares of the same material, which, when rotated 45 degrees, became decorative diamonds which helped to secure the larger panels where they join.

Maybeck specified planter boxes on the roof above the steel sash windows of the west elevation. Planters also topped the elaborate exterior ventilation ducts, structures which look convincingly like well-heads but are actually the extension of interior piers. Maybeck used overhead planters on other projects, including the

22

23

20 Square sheets of 'asbestos lumber' serve as exterior cladding, and are held in place by smaller red squares of the same material.
21 Interior concrete wall with rivulets caused by wrinkling of the paper lining the board forms.
22 Partial view of east elevation, taken from garden court between main church and Sunday School addition. Original standing seam sheet-metal roof later covered by tile roof.
23 Vine-laden trellis structures surmount each concrete column along the south elevation. Exposed beams supported by the capitals are extensions of the truss system on the interior of the Fireplace room.
24 West elevation, showing the planned integration of plantings and structure. The deep eaves are supported by carved beam ends which project through from the interior.

24

26

25

27

28

25 Detail of stone capital at Cluny, from Maybeck's sketchbook of French Romanesque churches, undated.

26 Capital at St Trophine, Arles.

27 Column detail in cathedral at Beaune, showing square-fluted shaft.

28 Detail of figure attached to column, from unidentified church.

29 South elevation columns with intricate build-up of trellis structure. Column shafts and figures show the influence of French Romanesque details recorded in Maybeck's sketchbook.

30 Cornerstone of the church with decorative features from early Christian architecture.

29

30

Leon L Roos house (1909) and the immense Palace of Fine Arts exhibition hall and rotunda for San Francisco's Panama-Pacific Exposition of 1915. The high planters at the palace were never used as intended, but the idea was to create the instant impression of a grand, Classical ruin. Similarly, at the church, the high planters were part of the landscaping plan to create the effect of an aged structure, and to mitigate the starkness of the concrete and factory-sash windows.

The planters were later removed, probably because they leaked or were difficult for a gardener to maintain. By the time they were deleted, however, the desired effect of overflowing greenery and blooms was already assured by wisteria which had climbed the height of four massive, 14 x 14in posts which flank the west tracery window. The posts are tied back to the transept by pairs of profiled rafters, the whole structure being surmounted by a delicate, multi-layered trellis. A smaller trellis carries the same vine the length of the eaves, assuring an abundant riot of colour in the spring.

On the south elevation, as shown in the presentation drawings, the elaborate columns of the trellis east of the portico are the visually-dominant element, positioned rhythmically between the expanses of steel sash. The square flutes of the columns are reminiscent of those in a detail sketch Maybeck made from the Burgundian cathedral of Beaune years before. The cast concrete capitals also derive, in spirit at least, from French Romanesque antecedents, possibly Ste Madeleine at Vézelay. But whatever their origin, the stooped, veiled figures, as if on pilgrimage to a healing, establish a convincing early Christian theme to reflect the underlying roots of Christian Science.

31

The entry: a calming transition

Covered walks along both entry axes offer areas of quiet approach to the interior of the church. Both major and minor points of access are open and direct, fulfilling the programme stipulation that the church should 'express welcome to all, exemplified in its entrance'. The longer, secondary approach from the west seems more of a charming discovery than a grand arrival. One is brought up almost to the elevation of the doorway by a short flight of steps from the sidewalk. A partially-covered pergola, with a trellis structure almost overcome with wisteria, leads past panels of industrial sash which illuminate the interior. The dim pergola soon terminates under the high freestanding portico. Directly ahead stand the doors to the original Sunday School (now known as the Fireplace room). Subtle devices – a step before the door, the lack of a dedicated gable or shed roof – scale back the importance of this entry in favour of its twin on the left.

Approaching the main entry from the south, along the gentle rise of the scored-concrete walk, the high portico creates a monumental space over the intersection of the axes. The exposed structure of the sheltering hood creates an outdoor vestibule where a brief pause comes naturally. The cornerstone tablet stands to one side, its cast-concrete lettering and lightly-pigmented frame catching the light from above. Originally, a small decorative fountain stood nearby. The main approach is compressed back to human scale by a low roof immediately over the entry doors. The overall progressive effect from street to door is quietly grand at first, then humbling, in preparation for the breathtaking revelation of the interior space.

An interior of carefully managed light, space and colour

Once inside, a small, low-ceilinged passage (later enclosed by a second set of doors) continues the feeling of compression begun by the gable roof over the door just outside. Moving towards the light of the narthex one begins to appreciate that the materials truly are the same inside as out. Sunlight is filtered through the blue–grey, hand-hammered panes of Belgian glass, sending broad sheets of light across the aisles at regular intervals. Skylights maintain the flow of sunlight to the narthex where the entry doors and Fireplace room intercept it on the Dwight Way side. Above the steel sash and concrete pillars, the low ceilings of the aisles are finished in rough-sawn sheathing, alternating 10 and 2in widths, nailed to 4 x 4in rafters. The wider boards are stained light grey, the narrower strips a darker blue-grey, setting up a polychrome rhythm echoed throughout the structure.[34]

To the right of the entry, and projecting back towards the street behind a sliding steel sash panel, is the original Sunday School, now aptly named the Fireplace room. It is a simple hall dominated by the monumental, vertically-oriented fireplace on the east wall. It would seem more like a dim, Gothic refectory but for the sunlight which floods in from the south-facing wall of glazed factory sash. The vernacular spirit of Maybeck's domestic architecture is clearly expressed here in the exposed roof

31 Southwest corner of the church today, sheltered by dense landscaping.
32 Main entry axis, flanked by trellis structures. Shadows from the high portico roof are cast in front of the entry doors.

33 Original Sunday School, now called the Fireplace room. Maybeck's Arts and Crafts period domestic design spirit predominates, from the massive chimney to the furnishings and lighting fixtures.

32

33

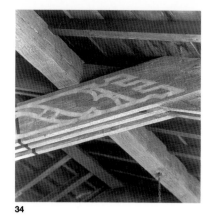

34

35

34 Fireplace room. Stencilled trusses are three boards which pierce the roof, then interlock with beams resting on south elevation columns.

35 First Reader's room. Maybeck designed chairs and tables for the Readers' rooms and board room situated behind the concrete screen and velvet panels at the front of the auditorium. Most of these pieces are now used in the Fireplace room.

36 Brightly decorated gable beams catch light from the south tracery window. At night, blue and red lights shine from the fixture (left) to illuminate beams and ceiling.

37 Looking south, afternoon light fills the west aisle of the auditorium.

36

37

structure and heavy presence of the chimney. Trusses, purlins and rafters are each stained a different hue, as if colour-coded according to purpose. A tracery design decorates the bottom chord of each truss, the centre of which is stained light grey to match the concrete of the chimney whose tapering shape at the same height is echoed by black outlines on the trusses. A home-like atmosphere is suggested by the simple Arts and Crafts redwood lighting fixtures – three-dimensional square crosses with metal caps and bare bulbs at the ends. In its current use as a meeting room, the table and chairs, all designed by Maybeck from English precedent, are gathered around the fireplace as naturally as if pulled up around the hearth at a friend's home.[35]

Across the narthex, on a diagonal opposite the Fireplace room, stands a bank of swinging oak doors which open to the spectacular main auditorium space. The simultaneous intimacy and majesty of this

vast hall is dreamlike, but the first impression – an overwhelming visual commotion of details – slowly gives way to reveal a coherent and highly-ordered decorative and structural system.

Maybeck's own words – 'the plan is the backbone of anything beautiful' – help to clarify an understanding of the interior and its complex and varied elements. The plan of the auditorium (as the main worship space is known in a Christian Science edifice) is a square or 'Greek' cross. Overhead, two clerestory levels form a volume of overlapping square crosses. The north end of these extends to accommodate the organ loft which rises to the highest roof level. To maximize the drama and practical use of the auditorium, Maybeck spanned the central space (40 ft²) with two pairs of crossed trusses, each a variation of the Pratt truss, patented by Thomas and Caleb Pratt in 1844. This was an unusual structural choice for a church interior, since Pratt trusses were used primarily for railroad bridges during the second half of the nineteenth century.[36] Here, a paired version of the trusses was designed to spring from each of four pentagonal piers which stand at the inside corners of the square cross plan. The piers carry the load of the massive trusses and are buttressed in turn by the clerestory walls which meet at a 90-degree angle at the backs of the piers.

Applied decoration as the exponent of structure

What appears to be decorative chaos in the auditorium in fact demonstrates a well-reasoned hierarchy. Christian Schneckenburger, the painting contractor hired to execute the delicate stencilling throughout the church, was a professional artist brought from New York to help prepare buildings for the expositions in San Francisco and San Diego of 1915. A sympathy clearly existed between Maybeck's design and Schneckenburger's execution of it. They understood each others talents and limitations. Maybeck praised Schneckenburger's work in the church, saying that he had 'made a wonderful job of it'.[37]

Overall, the decorative elements of the interior become richer and more expressive as they progress from floor to ceiling. At floor level, materials are left plain. The concrete piers, smooth at the bottom, become fluted only above the level of the pews. Painted decoration begins where the clerestory walls join the backs of the main piers. Triangular iron plates hold 10 x 10in Oregon pine posts in place, and a monochrome stencilled design overlaps both bracket and post to emphasize and celebrate the connection. Multi-coloured triangles at the tops of the piers' flutes form the transition to the elaborate cast-concrete capitals. The capitals themselves are nominally Romanesque in design, but include the Byzantine element of a rich palette of colour to brighten the woven basket shapes and swirling shafts of the miniature pilasters. The composition becomes even more complex above the capitals. Two layers of corbelled brackets and a layer of crossed blocks build up

38

39

to the spring-point for the trusses. In a characteristically romantic gesture, Maybeck reversed out his wife Annie's initials in the gold paint on each corbel.

At the clerestory height, the ceiling treatment becomes even more complex. The ceiling is dominated by gilt, profiled corbels which extend through the wall, past the ornate tracery windows to become rustic, unpainted exterior beams. Alternating 10 and 2in boards sheath the ceiling's background area as in the narthex and aisles, but groups of three 2 x 4in purlins, spaced three inches apart, take the place of the single 4 x 4in purlins on the lower ceilings. Progressing further up the decorative hierarchy, the major crossed trusses are boxed structural frames whose side and bottom lengths are filled with Gothic tracery panels, installed in continuous bands. Behind each panel, iron tension rods, the signature feature of the Pratt truss, are bolted to the bottom chords and fitted snugly into angled notches. This connection is emphasized by yet another stencilled design. The decorative tracery motif within each of the panels reflects the placement of the hidden tension rods: the reverse curve of the Gothic ogee describes the diagonal angle of the rods. Similarly, the vertical panels themselves correspond to the vertical compression posts of the truss. The multitude of gilded tracery panels catch the light from below, turning the otherwise dim truss and rafter area into a heaven of aurora-like reflections. Adding to this are more than 20 hanging 'pew lamps' suspended from the ceiling to a

height about 12ft above the floor. Intended to provide light for responsive readings, they also cast light through their trefoil cutouts to create a sea of delicate starlights. Above, the climactic intersection of the Pratt trusses – the point of greatest structural compression – is where Maybeck and Schneckenburger expended maximum decorative effort, expressing function as form at the literal and figurative high point of the auditorium.

The interior's north elevation is also dominated by Gothic tracery. A concrete screen, pierced with large quatrefoils, stands behind each of the two chairs on the dais behind the Reader's desk, located in the front of the auditorium where an altar would stand in a church of a different faith. Behind the screens, a panel of deep-burgundy velvet softens the hard predominance of concrete. The screens lend an aura of significance and consequence to the recitations of the two readers, but manage to do so without over-elevating

the status of the individuals themselves, as can often be the case in traditional pulpits. The base of the Reader's desk is also concrete, its coloured floral design deriving from a construction complication as the concrete was poured into board forms. These were lined with paper to ensure a smooth finished surface. The paper wrinkled in the process, however, causing indentations to run the height of the desk's base. Instead of ordering it to be filled or re-poured, Maybeck asked Schneckenburger to 'fix' it with paint. A charming decorative effect resulted in the most visible part of the church: the creases were artistically exploited to become tree trunks, with polychromatic branches painted directly on the concrete.[38]

38 Portion of main auditorium, looking south from the organ loft.
39 The main auditorium, looking east with the Reader's desk at left.
40 Interior detail of cast concrete capital with blocks and corbelled beams to support truss system. Note foul-air duct above capital, screened with a quatrefoil tracery panel.
41 Interior detail. Pratt trusses meeting above the centre of the auditorium. Colourful decorative stencilling symbolizes underlying hardware which stabilizes and fastens the junction. Tracery panels catch light cast by reflecting bowls below.
42 Buttressing side truss meets main truss, each containing Gothic ogee panels whose diagonal reflects the position of the iron tension rod behind it. Note black notches that secure the iron rods.

40

41

42

43

44

43 Centre aisle, looking south from the Reader's desk. An early plan for semi-circular seating was deleted in favour of one that allowed unobstructed views of everyone in the auditorium.

44 Sunday School addition designed in 1928 by Henry Gutterson in collaboration with Maybeck. A straightforward hall, the interior uses a decorative and structural vocabulary similar to the main church.

45 Interior, looking north, c1913. Note hanging metal stars at organ loft level. These were installed by church members but later removed reportedly because they created a distraction during services.

Above the Reader's desk a balcony rail, pierced with Gothic quatrefoils, conceals the organ console, behind which a gilt tracery screen supported by gold columns stands in front of the pipes. Late in life, Maybeck said he was unhappy with the screen in front of the pipes and even denied designing it.[39] It appears in the earliest archive photographs and blueprints, however, along with pressed-tin ornaments which were suspended like stars amid the tracery screen. Church members had hand-sewn the ornaments, attaching them to wires according to Maybeck's design, but they were ultimately removed reportedly because they distracted members during the services.

Maybeck had written that he favoured H H Richardson's Trinity Church, Boston (1873–7) above other churches.[40] He undoubtedly studied its square plan and lavish use of decorative colour on the interior, but it is a facile solution to suggest that Trinity, or any other structure, was the inspiration for First Church of Christ, Scientist. Trinity can be considered as one of the many antecedents which made an

A legacy of timeless beauty

Even if it were to be stripped of its prodigious decoration, Maybeck's auditorium would still define a noteworthy and dramatic space. But without the gilt tracery panels to give depth and life to the trusses, or the decorative stencilling to announce the structural functions, the space, if left undecorated, would have been merely rustic, or even gloomy. Instead, where materials meet, polychrome patterns celebrate the connection. Where structure is hidden, the opportunity is exploited to mark the place with a colourful statement. Strategic touches of blue, red, green and gold animate the wood, concrete and metal surfaces, vividly bringing to life Maybeck's playful sense of colour.

impression on Maybeck's work, but ultimately, First Church of Christ, Scientist is so fresh and wholly new that to belabour historical comparisons is to miss the point. Maybeck was creating straight from the heart. Inspired by the sincerity and creative instincts of the church membership, he designed as he did because he believed that those who had sought him represented a deep-seated faith which was beginning to reassert itself after a millennium's silence. The resulting edifice transcends period styles and spans the centuries as surely as Maybeck put himself, as he said, 'into the shoes of a twelfth-century man'.[41] Through the medium of concrete, steel sash and wood, First Church of Christ, Scientist is ultimately the legacy which most thoroughly expresses Maybeck's firmly-held belief in the ideal of beauty.

The Sunday School

In 1928, when Maybeck was 66, the church membership asked him to design a Sunday School structure to be contiguous with the main church on the east side. Henry Gutterson, a talented Berkeley architect and member of the church, was appointed architect in charge with Maybeck available to oversee. Maybeck claimed to have drawn the elevations.[42] The pastels which survive are unsigned, but they do bear the characteristic expressiveness and detailing of Maybeck's earlier drawings for the church.

45

The Sunday School wing extends east along Dwight Way, beginning with office space which backs up to the Fireplace room, then turns a right angle to the north at the Sunday School entry from the street. An exterior trellis structure nearly identical to the original for the main church continues along the sidewalk in front of the Sunday School addition, using the original molds to cast the distinctive capitals. The school's entry doors are carried out in a Gothic tracery design carved in wood and glazed with diamond-leaded art glass. Overhead stands a freestanding portico, a smaller version of the entry treatment for the main church. Inside, the philosophy of exposed structure and exuberant decoration is faithfully carried out. Many details are reminiscent of the main auditorium, which undoubtedly prepares young students for a comfortably familiar transition to the main building. The composite whole suffers, however, without the benefit of the arrestingly unusual volume and plan of the main church.

Despite his close involvement in the Sunday School, Maybeck complained that the lot was too narrow to do a proper job of the addition. The remark may have been calculated to distance himself from the final result, much as he had disowned the organ screen in the main auditorium when shown a picture of it in the 1950s. But whatever Maybeck's view, the addition is a sympa-thetically-designed space. It ultimately cannot compete, however, with its neighbouring source of inspiration, just as nearly any other structure would suffer in the same comparison – simply by reason of proximity.

The future of Maybeck's masterpiece
The membership of First Church of Christ, Scientist, Berkeley have continuously demonstrated their appreciation for the significance of the architecture they helped to create. Their respect for the building as a design achievement is as strong as their affection for the creative spirit of Bernard Ralph Maybeck. Maintenance and conservation of the building is assigned to a full-time professional and alterations, when undertaken at all, follow careful design criteria and are sensitively executed to honour the spirit of the original work. The firmest guarantee of the building's future as a church, however, is that its members understand now, as they did in 1910, how their edifice demonstrates the essential link between the material world and the metaphysical underpinnings of Christian Science. As a result, Bernard Maybeck's vision of faith as form perseveres as the greatest tribute to his art.

46

47

48

46 A venerable wisteria fulfills the original landscape plan as it wraps around massive trellis posts to root the structure literally and figuratively to its site.
47 East elevation from garden court. Pairs of exposed beam ends under the eaves are joined with filler blocks – carved members that do not extend to the interior but merely enhance the visual support of the projecting roof.
48 Main entry to Sunday School annex, with freestanding portico similar to main church entry.

Notes

1 Kenneth H Cardwell, *Bernard Maybeck: artisan, architect, artist.* Santa Barbara and Salt Lake City: Peregrine Smith, Inc., 1977, pp.13–16.

2 Bernard Maybeck, taped interview conducted by Robert Schultz in February 1953 for the radio station KPFA in Berkeley, California. Documents Collection, College of Environmental Design, University of California, Berkeley; hereafter cited as KPFA interview.

3 Cardwell op. cit. p.16.

4 Cardwell op. cit. p.17. Sara Boutelle, in her work on Julia Morgan, states that the Ecole des Beaux-Arts accepted only the top 30 applicants when Morgan tried for admission in 1897 and, successfully, in 1898. See Sara Holmes Boutelle, *Julia Morgan, Architect.* New York: Abbeville Press, 1988, p.30.

5 KPFA interview.

6 Sally B Woodbridge, *Bernard Maybeck: visionary architect.* New York, London, Paris: Abbeville Press, 1992, p.19.

7 ibid, p.20.

8 Richard Longstreth, *On the Edge of the World: four architects in San Francisco at the turn of the century.* New York: The Architectural History Foundation and Cambridge, Mass. and London: MIT Press, 1983, p.389 n. 28.

9 Leslie Mandelson Freudenheim and Elisabeth Sussman, *Building with Nature: roots of the San Francisco Bay region tradition.* Santa Barbara and Salt Lake City: Peregrine Smith, Inc., 1974, p.5.

10 Robert W Winter (ed.) *Arts and Crafts Architects in California.* Washington DC: Preservation Press, 1994 (forthcoming). See discussion of the Swedenborgian Church in the chapter entitled 'A C Schweinfurth'. See also Freudenheim op. cit. for an investigation of Worcester's influence.

11 Charles Keeler, *The Simple Home,* with a new introduction by Dimitri Shipounoff. Reprint of the first edition published by Paul Elder, San Francisco, 1904. Santa Barbara and Salt Lake City: Peregrine Smith, Inc., 1979, p.xxiii.

12 Keeler, Charles, *Friends Bearing Torches,* an unpublished manuscript of personal reminiscences begun in 1934, Keeler Papers, Bancroft Library, University of California, Berkeley, p.223.

13 Charles Keeler, *The Simple Home* op. cit. p.5.

14 Mary Baker Eddy, *Manual of The Mother Church: The First Church of Christ, Scientist in Boston, Massachusetts,* 89th edition, published by the Trustees under the Will of Mary Baker G Eddy, Boston, copyright 1895 and 1936, p.60.

15 Archives of First Church of Christ, Scientist, Berkeley, hereafter cited as Church archives. Minutes of the Board of Directors, 31 March 1905.

16 Church archives, minutes of the Board of Directors, 1 June 1905.

17 Church archives, minutes of the Plans Committee, a sub-committee of the Building Committee. In addition to Eulora M Jennings, a noted local artist, the Plans Committee included Helen P Smyth, Josephine S Snook, Elizabeth Watson (secretary) and Eleanor Juster.

18 Sara Holmes Boutelle, *Julia Morgan, Architect.* New York: Abbeville Press, 1988, p.30.

19 Church archives, notes kept by Eulora Jennings, chair of the Plans Committee.

20 Bernard Maybeck, from 'An interview with Mr Ralph Bernard (*sic*) Maybeck, architect of the edifice of First Church of Christ, Scientist of Berkeley, December 1953'. Typescript of a taped interview conducted by church members Don and Clara Owen. Church archives.

21 Rebecca Howell, 'Rebecca Howell interview'. Typescript of an interview recorded by church members Nadine Graham, Don Owen and Clara Owen on 1 March 1964. Church archives.

22 Church archives, Building Committee minutes, 27 March 1911 and Ruth Gordon, 'Partners in the book trade: Paul Elder and Morgan Shepard', *Quarterly News-Letter,* 43, spring 1982, p.36. I am grateful to Albert Sperisen and Ann Whipple of the Book Club of California for providing the latter.

23 Church archives. Undated, unsigned document which describes the needs and desires of the church membership with regard to their new church edifice. Hereafter cited as design programme. The handwriting appears to be the same as in other documents signed by Eulora Jennings.

24 Church archives, 'Report of the Plans Committee', dated 17 January 1910, signed by five members of the committee. The report defends the action taken to hire an architect, reminding the Building Committee of the motion passed by them: 'that the Committee on Plans be authorized to employ an architect or take such action as may seem wise to secure plans ... We regret that any misunderstanding should have arisen in the minds of the Building Committee ... It is of vastly more importance that we fit together as stone upon stone than that we have a material structure'.

25 KPFA interview. Maybeck's remarks on how he categorized his clients include: 'My customers are classified. I've tried to find out ... how I'm going to classify them historically ... starting with Gothic, [etc.]'.

26 Typescript of a taped interview with Maybeck, op cit.

27 Church archives, design programme.

28 The entry gate was executed but never installed. It is now in the collection of the Oakland Museum.

29 Church archives, minutes of the Building Committee.

30 Church archives, minutes of the Board of Directors.

31 Rebecca Howell interview.

32 Church archives, design programme. Maybeck was credited for inspiring some of the writing in the programme, possibly including this passage: '[the church] should express *sincerity* and *honesty* as exemplified in the use of genuine construction and materials which are what they claim to be and are not imitations in treatment or method of use of something else'.

33 Carbon copy of a letter dated 23 March 1910 from Maybeck & White, Architects, to Detroit Steel Products Company, Detroit, Michigan. Documents Collection, College of Environmental Design, University of California, Berkeley.

34 Church archives, contractor's specifications.

35 Church archives, Furnishings Committee notes and Building Committee minutes. These notes confirm that Maybeck designed the tables and chairs. Also, correspondence between A J Forbes & Son and C F Wieland (Documents Collection, College of Environmental Design, University of California, Berkeley) confirm that the furniture was manufactured by A J Forbes & Son, successor firm to Alexander Forbes who made the chairs for the San Francisco Swedenborgian Church in 1894. The Maybeck chairs closely resemble chairs made by English Arts and Crafts figure Ernest Gimson, after a design by Philip Clisett. Maybeck may have been aware of the Gimson chairs as they were widely exhibited in London and elsewhere during his travels for the University of California competition. See Mary Greensted, *The Arts and Crafts Movement in the Cotswolds.* Stroud, Glos. and Dover, New Hampshire: Alan Sutton Publishing Ltd, 1993, pp.13, 159, and ill. *94*.

36 Carl W Condit, *American Building.* Chicago and London: The University of Chicago Press, 1968, pp.96–7.

37 Owen interview; contains several of Maybeck's references to the quality of Schnekenburger's work.

38 Christian Schneckenburger's role in the painting of the Reader's desk base is recounted by Maybeck in the Owen interview. Maybeck related the story: 'I had to make [the Reader's desk] out of concrete, of course, and so as to make it smooth I put some tar paper on the inside and when I poured the concrete into it it made wrinkles, and then these wrinkles showed ... I told [Schnekenburger], "Now about those cracks that are there. Could you fix it?" So he used the cracks for branches and put leaves all over the branches. It made the loveliest possible kind of a picture'. Maybeck scholar Kenneth Cardwell questions this story, however, suggesting that the wrinkling was planned, or at least expected, and that Maybeck had conspired with Schnekenburger to create the effect.

39 In the Owen interview, Maybeck asserts that the screen in front of the organ pipes had been added. Maybeck's memory may have been failing, however, since the screen shows up on the original drawings and in the earliest extant interior photograph, taken before the interior appointments had been completed.

40 Woodbridge op. cit. p.91.

41 cf. note 25.

42 According to his own statements in the Owen interview, Maybeck drew the elevations, but Gutterson performed the balance of the design work for the 1928 Sunday School addition.

Previous page Main chimney, west elevation (the flue extension is not original). Coloured cathedral glass fills the industrial sash at organ-loft level.

Left Northwest corner at side entrance, showing the dynamics of the overhanging eaves at both clerestory levels.

Centre South elevation, showing freestanding cast-concrete columns surmounted by trellis structures. Profiled beam ends extend from interior truss chords in the Fireplace room.

Right The high main portico on the south elevation stands adjacent to a cast-concrete and wood pergola structure, which carries the wisteria vine as originally proposed.

Left East elevation from the garden court. Pairs of exposed beam ends under the eaves are joined with filler blocks – carved members that do not extend to the interior but merely enhance the visual support of the projecting roof.

Right Heavy structural elaboration is elevated to a design statement in Maybeck's scheme for the trellis and entry portico on the south elevation.

Left A pergola-covered walk from the southwest corner shelters the secondary entry axis. A giant sequoia, part of the original plan, dominates the structure.
Centre An ornate copper downspout to the right of the main entry doors reflects the architect's concern for comprehensive design control.
Right Main entry to the church, looking north from Dwight Way. The high portico, lush plantings and lack of stairs provide a welcoming and easy entry for everyone.

Main auditorium, looking north. Massive concrete piers support wooden blocks and corbels, which spring to the main truss system. Hammered-metal pew lamps and reflector bowls with trefoil cutouts cast light in all directions, picking out details in the gilded Gothic tracery panels overhead. The pervasive historically derived forms are enlivened and made entirely new by the exuberant use of colourful decoration.

Left The windowless upper clerestory level is dominated by gilded Gothic tracery panels set into the truss system.

Centre, above Colour-coded ceiling sheathing, purlins and rafters form a decorative structural backdrop for the main trusses and hanging light fixtures.

Centre, below A triangular iron bracket secures a timber post to its concrete pier base. Stencilled painting decoratively merges materials.

Right, above Gilded inside and unpainted outside, a series of paired beams – carved and separated by blocks – extend through the south tracery window to support the eaves.

Right, below Fireplace room. Stencilled triple truss chords pierce the roof to interlock with beams resting on the south elevation's trellis columns.

Left Nominally Romanesque, the cast-concrete capitals of the main interior piers also include Byzantine-inspired decorative accents of rich colour.

Right The capitals terminate in two layers of corbelled brackets and a layer of crossed blocks, built up to the spring-point for the trusses.

Left, above At the north end (front) of the auditorium, a gilt tracery screen springs from gold columns between the organ console and the pipes.

Left, below The south tracery window acts as a fanlight to flood the back of the auditorium with afternoon light.

Right Main auditorium, looking towards the southeast corner. The space forms a square, bi-axially symmetrical cross.

Left Creases in the paper-lined board forms caused unintended wrinkles in the concrete base of the Reader's desk. These were decorated to resemble tree trunks, with polychrome branches painted directly on the concrete.

Right On the dais behind the concrete Reader's desk, screens pierced with large quatrefoils rise to decorated spheres and blocks which in turn build up to support the organ-loft balcony.

Left Built-in music cabinet, a Maybeck design, is positioned between industrial sashes at the west end of the narthex.
Right West aisle, looking south. Post and beam structural composition allows natural light to flood auditorium through large expanses of steel sash filled with antique art glass.

Left Fireplace room, formerly the Sunday School. A home-like atmosphere is suggested by the simple Arts and Crafts redwood lighting fixtures, and by the table and chairs designed by Maybeck. The monumental chimney strongly recalls the architect's typical domestic designs.

Right First Reader's room. Below the organ loft at the north end of the structure, the small office is panelled in simple board and batten, and furnished with Maybeck's designs.

Left Entry, south elevation of the Sunday School addition, 1928. Similar to the main church, a portico rises over the approach to the entry doors and Gothic tracery appears in windows behind the narthex. Columns are cast from the original 1910 trellis column moulds.
Centre Interior detail of the Sunday School addition. Main piers terminate in tracery-panelled capitals, which hint of boxed Pratt trusses in the main auditorium.
Right Sunday School auditorium. The details and decorative exuberance are reminiscent of the main church, visually preparing young students for the transition to the adults' auditorium.

Architect's presentation renderings of (above) south elevation,
showing vine-covered pergola
and trellis structures much as
they still appear each spring, and
(below) west elevation
looking north, showing the
deep overhang of eaves.

The following drawings are based on Maybeck's own working drawings; some details were modified during construction.

Drawings

Location map

1 First Church of
   Christ, Scientist,
   Berkeley
2 University of
   California at Berkeley

Site plan

1 First Church of
   Christ, Scientist,
   Berkeley
2 Vedanta Society,
   Berkeley
3 University of
   California halls of
   residence
4 American Baptist
   Seminary of the
   West
5 University of
   California building
6 Private apartment
   building
7 People's Park

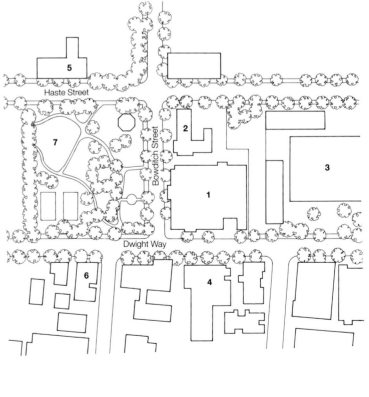

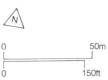

Floor plans

1 portico
2 pergola
3 entrance
4 narthex (lobby)
5 Sunday School
  (now called Fireplace room)
6 dressing room
7 main auditorium
8 aisle
9 Reader's desk
10 rear hallway
11 Usher's room
12 Board of Directors' room
13 First Reader's room
14 Second Reader's room
15 rear entrance
16 Janitor's room
17 office
18 side entrance
19 organ gallery

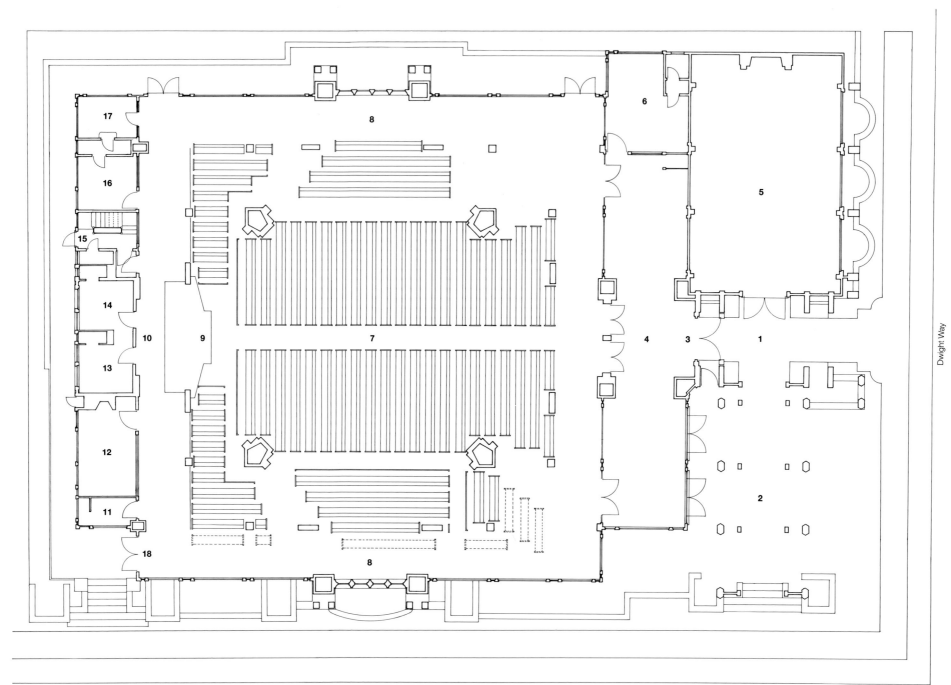

Ground floor

Bowditch Street

Dwight Way

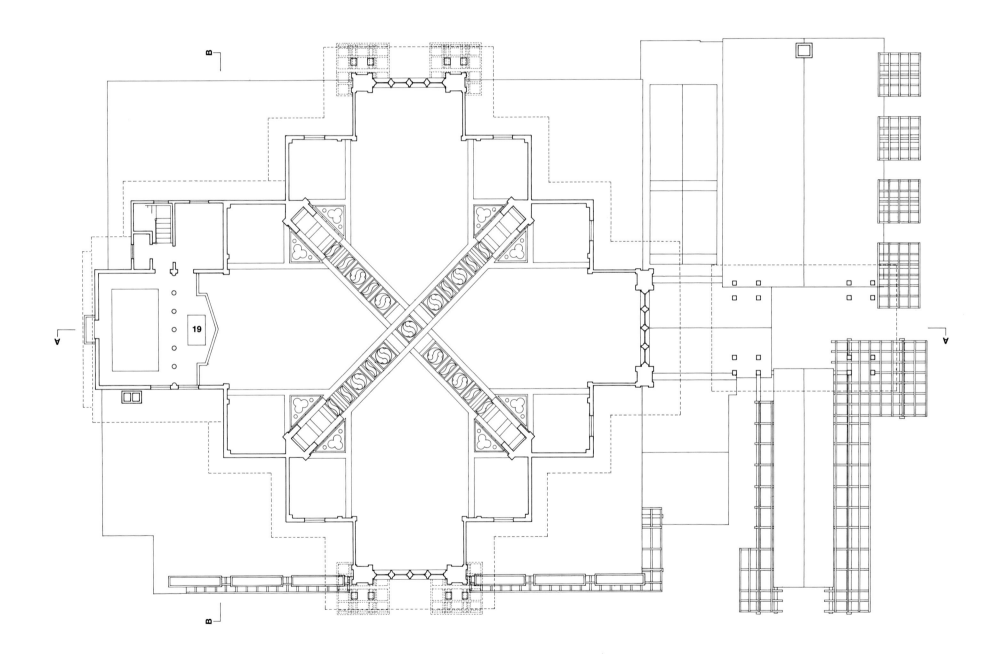

Clerestory level and reflected truss plan

Section AA

1 entrance portico
2 narthex (lobby)
3 aisle
4 main auditorium
5 Reader's desk
6 rear hallway
7 Second Reader's room
8 organ gallery

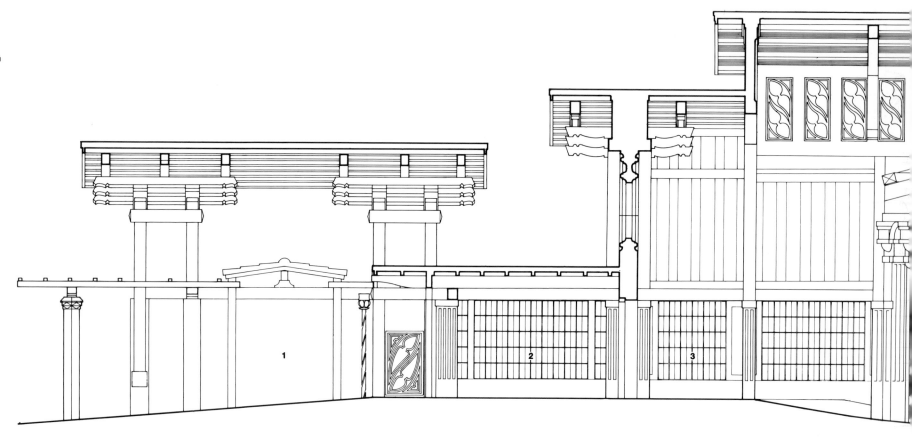

0   3m

0   10ft

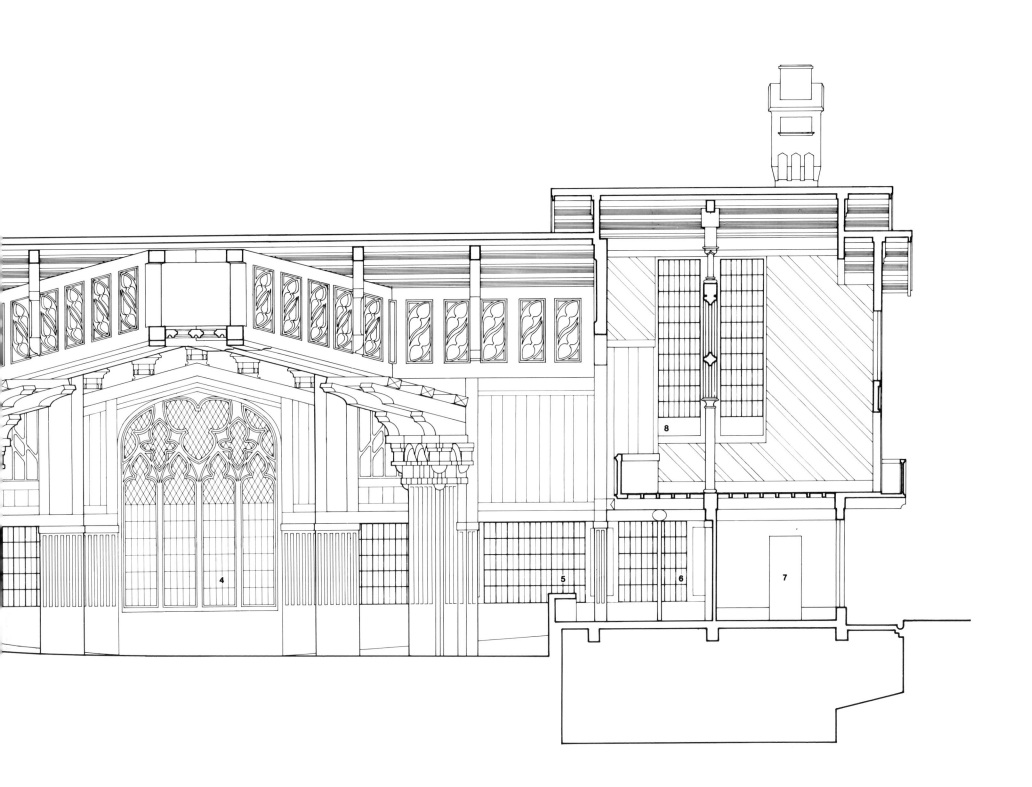

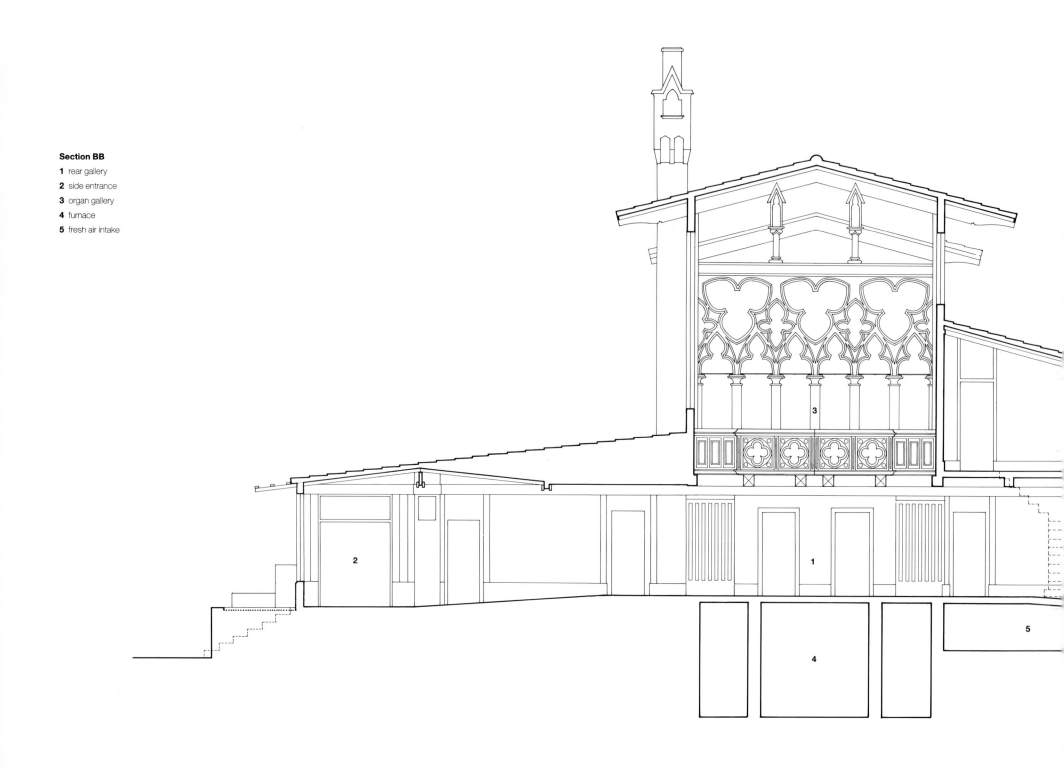

Section BB

1 rear gallery

2 side entrance

3 organ gallery

4 furnace

5 fresh air intake

0   3m

0   10ft

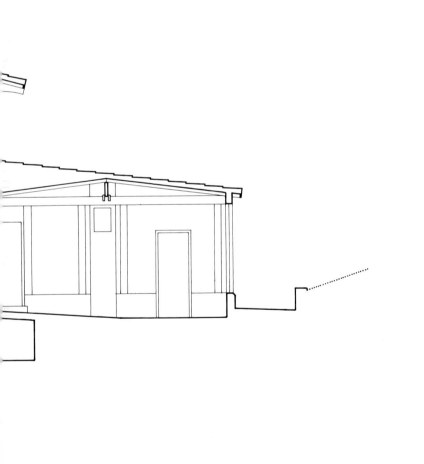

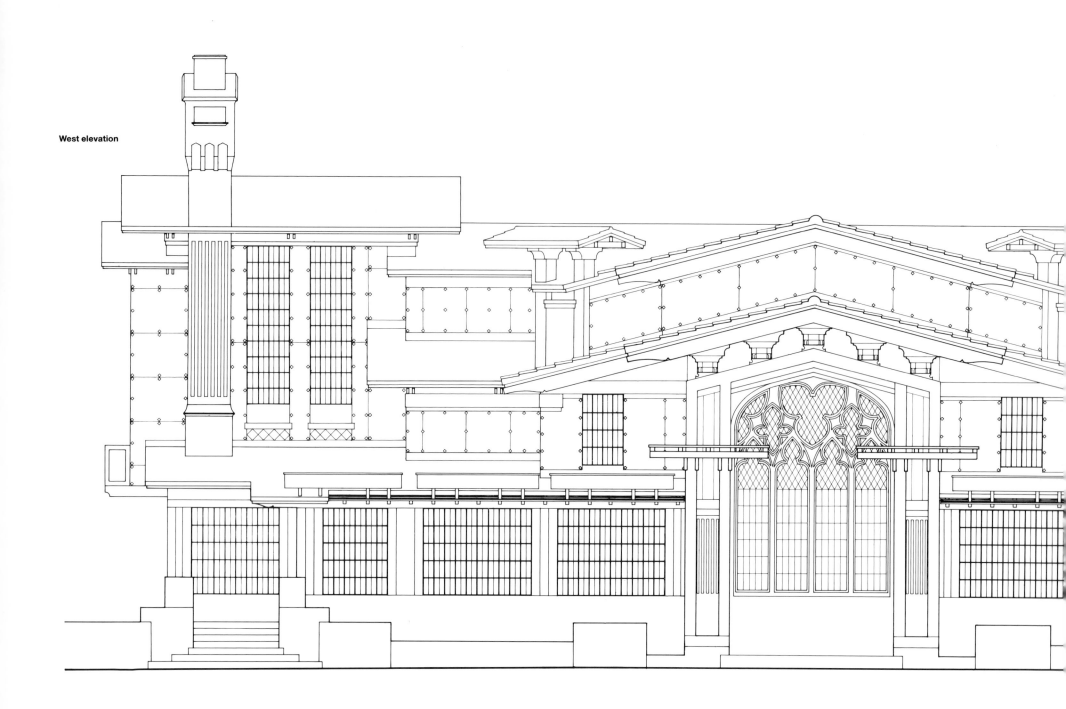

West elevation

0   3m

0   10ft

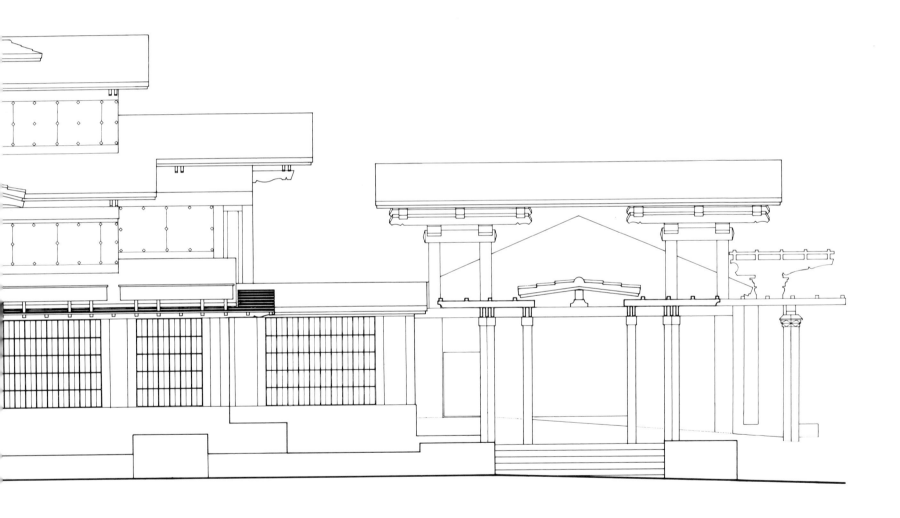

South elevation

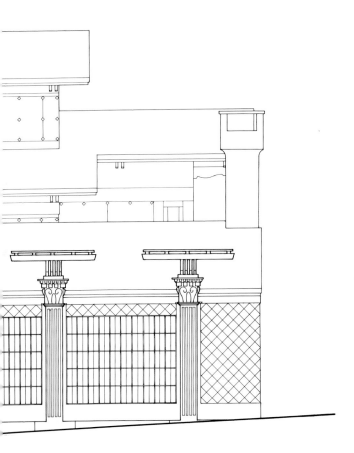

For Kirby and Will

Author's acknowledgements

I would like to thank the following individuals who helped signifi-cantly in the production of this book: William Marquand, of Stephen E Harriman AIA & Associates, who supported the project among the membership of the church and whose Foreword puts Maybeck's art into context with Christian Science; John Howell Jr, whose recollections of his parents' close association with the building of the church led to new information; John Gaul, whose familiarity with Maybeck, his family and friends was of significant interest and value; the late Florence Jury, who gener-ously contributed previously unpublished photographs of Maybeck; Jacomena Maybeck, whose delightful hospitality and willingness to share personal rec-ollections made for pleasurable research; Kristen Kwan, who was an invaluable help at the Documents Collection at the College of Environmental Design, University of California, Berkeley; Bruce Smith, who shared my enthusiasm and introduced me to Ethiopian food; Charles Dickinson, who shared his con-siderable knowledge of the build-ing and who helped with the site plan; Grace Reinenman, who shared important reminiscences; Ken Cardwell, whose critical pen-cil and insights improved the text; Sally Woodbridge, for reading the manuscript and offering her sup-port; and the membership and Executive Board of First Church of Christ, Scientist, Berkeley who were interested, friendly and cooperative; thank you all.

Illustration credits

The following illustrations are reproduced courtesy of: Documents Collection, College of Environmental Design, University of California, Berkeley: 6, 10, 16, 25; Florence Jury: 1, 2; First Church of Christ, Scientist, Berkeley: 14, 17, 48; *The Christian Science Journal*: 9; William S Ricco: 7.

Chronology

7 February 1862 Bernard Ralph Maybeck is born in New York City to Bernhardt and Elisa Maybeck.

March 1882 Maybeck passes the examination to enter the Ecole des Beaux-Arts, Paris.

29 October 1890 Maybeck marries Annie White of Kansas City, Mo.

1891 Maybeck joins the staff of architect A Page Brown in San Francisco and contributes to the design of the California Building for the World's Columbian Exposition to be held in Chicago in 1893.

1894 Maybeck assists Brown and Schweinfurth with the Swedenborgian Church design, then leaves the office to accept a teaching position at the University of California as instructor in draw-ing. The cornerstone is laid at The First Church of Christ, Scientist, Boston, Massachusetts, also known as The Mother Church.

1895 Maybeck designs a house for Charles Keeler, his first client as an independent architect.

1896 Maybeck persuades Phoebe Apperson Hearst to sponsor an international competi-tion to select a master plan for the University of California campus in Berkeley, California.

20 August 1897 A Christian Science meeting is held informally in Berkeley for the first time.

27 March 1905 A charter is issued to First Church of Christ, Scientist, Berkeley. Meetings con-tinue to be held in temporary quarters, but discussions begin immediately regarding the pur-chase of land for a permanent church edifice.

24 August 1909 The first meet-ing of the Plans Committee to dis-cuss hiring an architect is held. The committee visits architects in San Francisco that afternoon, probably making their initial visit to Maybeck at that time. A budget is set at a minimum of $25,000, with no maximum.

27 September 1909 The Building Committee votes to hire Maybeck as architect upon rec-ommendation of the Plans Committee.

17 January 1910 Maybeck sub-mits colour perspective drawings to the Building Committee.

February–September 1910 C F Wieland is hired from the church membership to super-vise construction and to liaise between the Building Committee and architect's office. Requests for bids are released. Contractors and sub-contractors are chosen.

26 September 1910 A building permit is issued.

16 August 1911 The first service is held in the new church struc-ture using rented chairs.

March 1912 Pews are installed in the auditorium.

26 December 1916 Dedication of the First Church of Christ, Scientist, Berkeley takes place with special services which rec-ognize that the debt undertaken for the building of the church has been lifted. The final cost of con-struction and furnishings was approximately $60,000.

20 January 1929 The new Sunday School edifice is opened adjacent to the main church building. Cost: approximately $60,000.

1951 Maybeck is awarded the Gold Medal of Honor, the highest recognition accorded by the American Institute of Architects.

3 October 1957 Bernard Ralph Maybeck dies.

Select bibliography

The following is a partial listing of books and articles in which First Church of Christ, Scientist, Berkeley is mentioned or described.

Bangs, Jean Murray (Mrs Harwell Hamilton Harris), 'Bernard Ralph Maybeck, archi-tect comes into his own', *Architectural Record*, 103, January 1948, pp.72–9.

Cardwell, Kenneth H, *Bernard Maybeck: artisan, architect, artist*. Santa Barbara and Salt Lake City: Peregrine Smith, Inc., 1977, pp.119–32. Cardwell describes the church as 'the visible state-ment of [Maybeck's] design phi-losophy at its most fruitful stage,' and notes that 'in the Christian Science church there is a sym-bolic coordination of ornament and structure'.

'Maybeck's mood: Christian Science church in Berkeley', *Architectural Forum*, 115, July 1961, pp.103–6.

Jordy, William H, *Progressive and Academic Ideals at the Turn of the Century*. New York and Oxford: Oxford University Press, 1972, pp.300–12. Jordy describes the church as showing 'the Imperial side of Maybeck,' and calls the square cross plan a 'formal, hierarchical organiza-tion congenial to Beaux-Arts monumentality'.

McCoy, Esther, *Five California Architects*. New York: Reinhold, 1960. Reprinted New York: Praeger, 1975. This important early study of California architec-ture brought a rational under-standing of key figures to a broad audience for the first time. McCoy treats Maybeck's Christian Science church with realism and sympathy stating, 'No one has ever carried the burden of the past more weightlessly'.

Starr, Kevin, *Americans and the California Dream*. Santa Barbara and Salt Lake City: Peregrine Smith, Inc., 1981, p.297. Starr credits Maybeck for 'wanting a new, distinct California idiom, a blending of free form wood and stone, an architecture that was organic, fond of color, open to sun, expressive of landscape ...'.

Woodbridge, Sally B, *Bernard Maybeck: visionary architect*. New York, London, Paris: Abbeville Press, 1992, pp.89–98. Woodbridge accurately conjures up the mixed signals sent by Maybeck in the church design: 'Even more complex in its imagery than Maybeck's other works, First Church of Christ, Scientist beggars description and must be seen to be comprehended'.

3 ARCHITECTURE s

ARTS & CRAFTS MASTERPIECES

Beth Dunlop is the former architecture critic of the *Miami Herald* and currently writes on architecture for a variety of publications.

Edward Prior
St Andrew's Church, Roker

Trevor Garnham studied History of Art under Joseph Rykwert and Dalibor Vesely at the University of Essex before entering practice as an architect. He is currently Senior Lecturer at Kingston University School of Architecture. He has a special interest in the writings of John Ruskin and has written on the work of late Victorian architects such as Deane and Woodward and F.W. Troup. He is author of *Oxford Museum* in the Architecture in Detail series.

Charles Rennie Mackintosh
Glasgow School of Art

Dr James Macaulay is Senior Lecturer in architectural history at the Mackintosh School of Architecture, Glasgow. He has been chairman of both the Society of Architectural Historians of Great Britain and the Architectural Society of Scotland. He is author of *The Gothic Revival, 1745–1845* and *The Classical Country House in Scotland, 1660–1800* and contributed to *Mackintosh's Masterwork: The Glasgow School of Art* and *Charles Rennie Mackintosh: The Architectural Papers*.

Acknowledgements The author could not have written this book without the help of many people, in particular the staff of the library of the Glasgow School of Art, especially Mrs Margaret Duff, Mr George Rawson and Mr Neil McVicar and Mr David Buri, the former and present architectural librarians. Mr Peter Trowles, the curator of the Mackintosh Collection at the Glasgow School of Art, generously made available his discovery in the summer of 1992 of a box containing many documents including letters from C.R. Mackintosh and his 'Description and Schedule of Contents', which formed part of the competition submission. Although these papers do not alter the history of the building, they add much detail to the story. The main archive relating to Mackintosh is held at the Hunterian Art Gallery, the University of Glasgow, where Mrs Pamela Robertson has given advice and encouragement to scholars over many years. The gallery's collection was enriched by the gift of S.B.T. Keppie of the books of Mackintosh's firm. The photographs of the Mackintosh drawings were prepared by Mrs Carvalho and Mr F. Macmillan. Drawings, among which are the office copies for the second stage of the Glasgow School of Art dated 1907, were examined by courtesy of Mr William Hardie of William Hardie Ltd. Finally, a debt of thirty years can now be paid to Mr Tom Gardner since it was he who first encouraged the author to write about Mackintosh.

Text illustrations are reproduced with the permission of the following: The Architectural Press (2, 3, 6, 9, 10 and 52); Mackintosh Collection, Hunterian Art Gallery, University of Glasgow (4, 5, 7, 16 and 51); Glasgow School of Art (12); National Monuments Record (29 and 47); Scottish National Buildings Record (32 and 39) and the Royal Commission on the Ancient and Historical Monuments of Scotland (46).

Bernard Maybeck
First Church of Christ, Scientist, Berkeley

Edward R. Bosley is Associate Director of the Gamble House. He holds a degree in History of Art from the University of California at Berkeley, where he studied the work of the Greenes first-hand, living for several years in one of their classic, high-period commissions, the W.R. Thorsen House (1909). He also holds a Masters degree in Management from the University of California at Los Angeles and has written and lectured extensively on the work of Greene and Greene.

Phaidon Press Limited
Regent's Wharf
All Saints Street
London N1 9PA

Arts & Masterpieces first published 1999
© 1999 Phaidon Press Limited
ISBN 0 7148 3876 4

A CIP catalogue record for this book is available
from the British Library.

Printed in Hong Kong

St Andrew's Church, Roker originally published in
Architecture in Detail series 1996
© 1996 Phaidon Press Limited
Photography © 1996 Martin Charles, unless
otherwise stated
Glasgow School of Art originally published in
Architecture in Detail series 1993
Reprinted 1993
© 1993 Phaidon Press Limited
Photography © 1993 Mark Fiennes, unless
otherwise stated
First Church of Christ, Scientist, Berkeley originally
published in Architecture in Detail series 1994
© 1994 Phaidon Press Limited